Reaching Out with No Hands

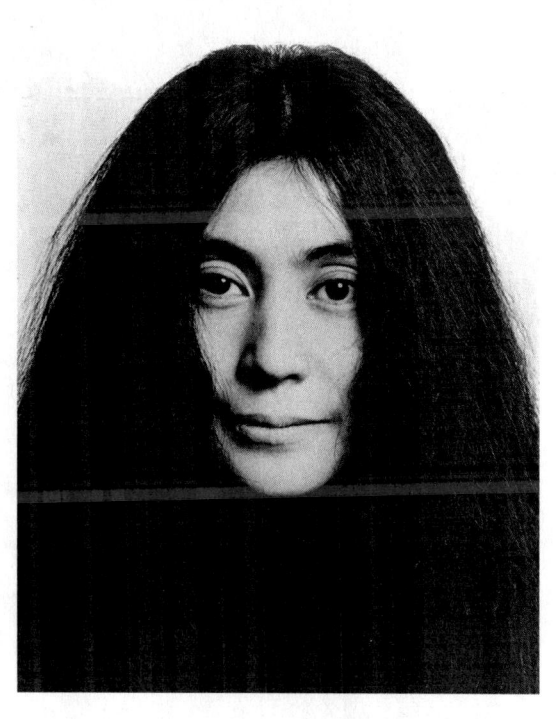

Reaching Out with No Hands

RECONSIDERING YOKO ONO

LISA CARVER

An Imprint of Hal Leonard Corporation

Copyright © 2012 by Lisa Carver

All rights reserved. No part of this book may be reproduced in any form, without written permission, except by a newspaper or magazine reviewer who wishes to quote brief passages in connection with a review.

Published in 2012 by Backbeat Books
An Imprint of Hal Leonard Corporation
7777 West Bluemound Road
Milwaukee, WI 53213

Trade Book Division Editorial Offices
33 Plymouth St., Montclair, NJ 07042

Photo of Yoko Ono © Photofest.
Book design by UB Communications

Printed in the United States of America

Library of Congress Cataloging-in-Publication Data is available upon request.

ISBN 978-1-61713-094-6

www.backbeatbooks.com

For Mike Edison

CONTENTS

Your Very Name, a Curse 1

What Is Not Yoko Ono 3

Some Pieces 25

There Were Fights 27

Pretty 29

Despair and Loneliness, or, What it Felt Like to Be an Asian Woman Trying to Make Art and Make Her Way in America, 1960 31

Fluxus 33

Devil's Advocate . . . Except She'd Probably Argue with Him, Too 37

Burning 39

Cut 41

Bag 47

To Lose Is to Save 49

Earthquake Baby 53

Yoko Said 57

The $3000 Apple 59

Yoko and the Blues 61

Nail 65

What Is the Sound of No Hands Clapping? 69

Just Before the Silence 71

John Backed Her Up When She Said There Was Good in Hitler and Every Living Thing	73
East and West	83
What a Mother Should Be	85
What a Good Voice Hides	89
Proof	91
But Is It Good?	93
Surprise!	95
Like What Your Elbow or Knee Feels Like When You're Thrown Off a Motorcycle and Slide Ten Feet	97
Messing Up the Old Rockers, Shaking Up the Old Rock	99
Live Peace in Toronto, 1969	103
Chuck Berry Was Shocked	105
Bastard	107
Men	109
John Ripped *Her* Off!	111
A Film Called *Rape*	113
Equal Opportunity	117
Out	119
Lonely	123
Money	125
A Born Widow	127
Girlfriend	131
People as Art	133

Monster	135
What a Stepmother Should Be	137
Still Making People Mad After All These Years	139
Remember	143
Life Is Beautiful	147
I Just Don't Know What to Say About This	149
Wishing's for Suckers	151
Ambassador of Autism	153
Selected Bibliography	155

Reaching Out with No Hands

YOUR VERY NAME, A CURSE

When Kate Hudson got together with multiplatinum rock band Muse's front man, Matt Bellamy, his bandmates reportedly called her Yoko Ono—though when contacted, they vehemently denied it, saying they would never "insult their best friend's wife like that."

To call someone Yoko Ono, this incredible transgressive artist active for sixty years in a dozen countries, a woman who has recorded close to twenty albums, and creating as many different art exhibitions, films, books, and social activist campaigns, is an *insult*? Of course, in our indelicate, gossip-driven culture, few could name even one song or work of art of the thousands she has done. Instead, what most people "know" about this artist is that she broke up the Beatles, is pretty much the ugliest woman in the world, and there's some vague recollection that her daughter was kidnapped, which she kind of deserved, due to being on drugs and neglectful, too busy hypnotizing John Lennon with voodoo heroin sexuality and reading tarot cards instead of mothering and normal good-wiving.

In *Esquire* magazine in 2010, Yoko looked back on being called Dragon Lady, and all the blaming energy aimed at her, as "trying to erase me." But eventually she came to be thankful for the "incredible power" used against her, because she was able to absorb it and use it to become more powerful herself, or to make bigger things. "Power is power. It's energy. And if you get big, big energy, you can use that...." In her song "Revelations," she sings: "Bless you for your anger; it's a sign of rising energy. Bless you for your greed; it's a sign of great capacity." And she did use all the negative energy, like it was a rain of bullets aimed at her and she caught them in her bare hand and popped each one in her mouth and swallowed, for the iron.

She uses her emotions; she uses her life; she uses her family's lives—recordings of her husband on the telephone, her dying baby's heartbeat.

She uses the audience to complete her ideas—they had to "see" for themselves the dance Yoko had choreographed for dancers on a stage in complete darkness. For one piece she did (in 1961 and again in 2010), the audience member had to scream into a waiting microphone while Yoko remained silent.

She uses a beam of light (literally) to express her ideas. She has a *Whisper Piece*. She has a *Shadow Piece*. For her medium, she uses billboards, trees, wishes.

She used the very media that tried to erase her ideas to disseminate her ideas a thousandfold.

No mention was made that *Esquire* was the same publication that, forty or so years earlier, ran a feature on the artist with the astonishing title "John Rennon's Excrusive Gloupie."

WHAT IS NOT YOKO ONO

This book is not about Yoko Ono. It's about what she isn't. What she doesn't do, and what she will not be.

Yoko Ono is not pretty, she is not easy, her paintings aren't recognizable, her voice is not melodious, her films are without plot, and her Happenings make no sense. One of her paintings you are told to sleep on. One of her paintings you are told to burn. One of her paintings isn't a painting at all—it's *you* climbing into an outdoor bathtub and looking at the sky. Most of her stuff is not even there. This is why I love her. This is why we need her. We have too much stuff already. It clutters our view, inward and outward. We need more impossible in our culture.

Go out and capture moonlight on water in a bucket, she commands. Her art is instructions for tasks impossible to complete. We already have a billion lovely things and a million amazing artists who have honed their talent and have lorded it above us. People who have achieved the highest of the possible. People wearing their role as artist or writer or filmmaker or spokesperson as a suit of armor or an invisibility cloak or an intimidatingly, unacquirably tasteful outfit. Even other artists can't figure Yoko out or accept her as legit, nor can she obey the club rules. Her stuff is all wrong. Grow a weed and admire it. "Listen" to a two-minute song of recorded silence, music lovers. And you, the most imperialist and arms-profiteering superpower in the history of the world, give peace a chance.

When you tell someone to do the undoable, you're really only showing them how impossible it ever was that anyone wanted us to use our lifetime to follow orders, to accept what is agreed is reasonable. We already have a million people telling us what to do and what to believe. Yoko is telling us, "You don't have to."

She proposes the idea that all we thought *had* to be done didn't have to, doesn't have to. And maybe some exploitative things we did to maintain order, our position on the job and in the family, were not necessary and normal after all. Life might not be arranged along one certain pyramid of hierarchal order.

These propositions are most threatening to the ones who have believed in the existing order the strongest, and tamped down their doubts the hardest. Men are vehement in talking about how ugly she is. They say it like her face is assaulting them. A friend of mine—a Republican—came over and was chewing on a pretzel and he made me turn my Yoko Ono book the other way so he didn't have to see her face while he was eating. He thought this great feeling of disturbance emanated from a photograph from forty years ago! *No one* is that hideous, and certainly not Yoko Ono! This extreme hostile reaction is insane! Who feels threatened from just looking at someone's face on the cover of a book? It must have been the message in the face that made my friend lose his appetite: the look in Yoko's eye, the set of her mouth, the fall of her hair, along with what little he knew or felt about her as an artist and a person. Somehow it made him question himself. And his defensiveness quickly turned to offense.

In fact, her face is beautiful. Noble and powerful. But somehow it just doesn't *fit*. It doesn't make sense like other faces do, doesn't follow the rules of comportment: makeup and expression. You can't skip over it and not really see it, like with regular pretty faces. (The same with her voice.) Something about it arrests you... but what is it about it?! The eyes hold you. They have history, they have iced-over pain. They are holes and you don't know how far down they go, and you might fall in.

Her voice, too, is not not beautiful, exactly. It just doesn't fit right, either. She sings these powerful exhortations or gripping descriptions with that whispery or reedy voice. It sounds too small to carry the weight of what it's saying. And sometimes it's just naked emotions grunted or wailed out and it feels indecent. It's too *different*. Listening, we feel unsettled, and then we get angry that someone made us feel unsettled. People are supposed to entertain or soothe us with their song, and instead she stirs us up and then just leaves us there confused and feeling we don't know what.

"Let water drop," begins Yoko's instructional painting *Waterdrop*. "Place a stone under it. The painting ends when a hole is drilled in the stone with the drops."

How do you measure the success of a conceptual artist's work, when the most important part takes place in the minds of others? What Yoko Ono does is plant seeds of doubt. Doubt that things are as we have been told, as we have always believed. Doubt that war is necessary. That women are emotional and fragile and therefore should not be leaders. That punishment is the answer. That we can't sing, that we have bad voices. She plants these seeds and a few will grow into trees maybe ten, twenty, a hundred years later. And they'll all be different, because the trees are the new ideas that grow in the space where the old ideas had been crowding our brains.

So then how do you measure the success of the conceptual artist in her own lifetime? I suppose by how unsolid they are able to remain, despite all the pressure to conform, to put something down that can be reproduced and mass-marketed. The pressure to complete something, and thereby turn your back on trusting other people to successfully complete your work. In that sense, concerning her own work, I believe Yoko Ono may be the most loyal there has ever been to keeping her message in the realm of the unattainable, unhaveable.

Yes, there were forays into creating somewhat traditional songs, things of beauty and wholeness. But those exceptions prove the rule, and besides, music remains fluid no matter what—you can never hold it. But even then, those songs—like 1982's ocean wave-like "Dream Love" or 1981's melancholy and tremulous "Goodbye Sadness" or 1972's perfectly controlled ember-y angry glowering wolf of a song "Death of Samantha"— were more like postcards sent from the depths of banishment, or promises to herself, mantras. That's how outer she is—she's even outside what she is, and her most inside-the-norm creations are about being outside. Yet she keeps coming back for us. She does, day after day, half century after half century, what it is an artist does: come back for us. Not to show us the way (her way), but to remind us that we already know the way out of our troubles; just take it. Just wish for it, and it will open up. Everything is all right. Even the pain. Even the loneliness. Everything is right.

Yoko remains liquid, yet she simply will not follow the rules of the elements and seep into the background. She doesn't blend in, settle. She is not ignorable. She remains distinct, outside. She does not slip into the mythology of the song; she remains demandingly human. Yoko's "Walking on Thin Ice" has the same cold music and removed lyrics of New Order's "Blue Monday," but something in Yoko's voice does not allow us to forget her, the woman singing, the way we go into the song and forget the man with the voice in New Order. She remains obstinately, inconveniently alive at all times, in all that she does.

She is the most important disrespected artist—bringer of strange new communication—of the last hundred years. "We are all together in this world," she says to war-happy Li'l Abner cartoonist and newspaper columnist Al Capp, one of the journalists invited to Yoko's and John's Bed-In in Canada in 1969. She said to him: "You and I are married." She is trying to show connectedness to him, even though he is supposedly her enemy. He needs to keep the separation; he protects his bigotry because, I think, he's afraid he will get lost without it, without the clear markers of who he is and who he isn't. He calls her Madame Nhu several times, he calls her hirsute, he says why don't you go to Saigon, he responds to her declaration that we are all married "a very unkind thought to plant in my mind. I may wake up screaming. It's a matter of taste." He carries on, and interrupts her every time she attempts to answer one of his (not wanting an answer) questions, often addressing himself to John Lennon instead. "Good God, you gotta live with *that*?!" he says in reference to John's bride on their honeymoon. "I feel sorry for you." Yoko ignores the insult and continues to try to exchange meaning: "Me is you and you is me." There is cross talk on the video, so I can't understand exactly what he says next, but it's something like: "I don't permit you to speak for me. I'll choose Marilyn Monroe, not Madame Nhu. Whatever race you're the representative of, I ain't a part of it." John's anger rises, but Yoko is accepting. She lights a cigarette, leans back. She is used to this—to people clinging to their perception of her as Other, no matter how far she reaches to show we're Same. She can bide her time. She is not knocked off course. She knows her very understanding of connection makes her alien. She keeps her gaze fixed on the gods inside—deep, deep inside—the barbarians.

Such fierceness she evokes, even today—of thrill or disgust. These reactions must come at her like bombs. She seems impervious to it, and yet there is a fragile element to Yoko that makes one feel protective. But then, what to do with the confrontational element equally there? Very aggressive and powerful and brave. Should I have sympathy or admiration or worry about what she might reveal about me to me? There is something defiant to her, and at the same time wounded... like the injured chick that the others will peck to death if they notice the injury, and she flaunts hers. She's not afraid of us. Why isn't she?

She knows how different she is, and she knows how annoying the different is to the human mind, which gravitates toward sameness for reassurance. That is why she gave herself the nickname the Fly. She said, at seventy years old, that she'd never thought the world would accept her in her lifetime. Can you imagine feeling so outside everything that you think you will *never* be understood? What freedom!

Yoko has always been outside, even as a child. She was born rich; then the war turned her into a beggar; then the family moved to America and she was rich again, but now she was a foreigner. As an artist, she was unknown and then she was known and hated; she was powerless and then she was bursting with power, but a borrowed power, at a price. In the first part of her career, she was misunderstood and neglected and ridiculed even by her own kind, and then she was sought out and begged to, as a pathway, for her connection to Lennon. She was never one of them. She was not even one of her own kind. She was not even one of the things that she is! Nor is she what she is not. While it can be said that she and her work are not pretty or easy or recognizable, they also *are* all these things, very much so! She is a transforming target.

In the latter half of her career, she finally became an icon for various subcultures, but what or where exactly is *her* culture or clique or movement? She will meld with club DJs for a while, or go onstage with an alternative-youth feedback master, but they are none of them her genre. They are picking her up like an exotic instrument, like a didgeridoo, and then they put her down again.

Every time Yoko's fortune and class changed, she was treated totally differently, but she was always the same. When you grow up that uncertain and sensitive to hypocrisy, and as an adult see the pattern repeating, you seek to create uncertainty in order to expose any possible hypocrisy, for which you are hypervigilant.

She is careful to not be swallowed, but at the same time remains open and fluid to blend with whatever new force comes along to briefly merge with hers. Musically, she was lost, and then she was "found," in 1992, when her six-CD *Onobox* rereleases came out on the Rykodisc label for all the people who weren't ready for her records when they were originally released in the 1970s. She collaborated with alternative musicians in the '90s, and in the 2000s, her songs were made into dance mixes for clubbers. Asked about how she adapted to the Internet and iTunes, she said, "I didn't have any kind of resistance with it and it's worked wonderfully." In all the collaborations she's done, way back to the early '60s with Ornette Coleman, right up to 2007's "Yes, I'm a Witch," where the likes of the Flaming Lips, Jason Pierce of Spiritualized and Spacemen 3, Cat Power, and Peaches remixed and replayed and re-sang with Yoko on her old songs, she's always Yoko Ono. Not since Johnny Cash has an artist blended throughout her career so thoroughly with contemporaries and young'uns alike, yet remained convincingly herself. No matter who Yoko works with throughout her career, she is never drowned out, or turned into something else amidst the collective, yet she is also very accessible to change, to the new influence; no "resistance" shows. But it's there. Or else how would she always stay herself. It's just, what is she? I don't know.

I can't place exactly what she is. But I am so inspired by what she's not.

Yoko's art is not to give us something to look at or listen to, and her activism is not to give us what to think. It's to get us to stop seeing what we're seeing and stop hearing what we're hearing and stop knowing what we're knowing, because all that gets in the way of what's really there. Her revolutionary personal life is not a model to envy or emulate. It's an exhortation to not mindlessly perform our various roles simply because that's "how it's done," but to do instead what we really want to, how we really want to. Untie your mind! And your eyeballs! And your earholes! And your heart! They're all in knots!

We're being used. We're slaves. We're drafted. Did you know it? Do you feel it? No? Feel harder. Or maybe easier. All the things we don't question, because we were not told there is a choice. We need a guide to come back for us and show us that where we thought was a wall is a door.

She is like LSD. LSD lets us see and feel what we'd been filtering out, the stuff that is inconvenient to see, or distracting us from our jobs and social demands. Not only do we get the epiphany on acid that the carpet is not solid, but also that habits aren't either, nor a belief system. It's all alive and breathing and ready—eager!—to change shape.

Which is why LSD is illegal, despite its having been successfully used to treat alcoholism. They don't want you awake in your own life. Alcohol is like TV, it keeps workers working, and LSD is like turning off the TV. People quit. If you see what's really there, you'd be so admiring, you'd have no time to work, no inclination to get ahead or to prepare your children for work. Because life is so beautiful. (Of course, you also might not get out of the way of an oncoming truck.)

Yoko's art, too, is not its own thing so much as a conduit through which awakening pours, different in every one of us.

In 2010, at the Museum of Modern Art in New York City, she walked out into the atrium and—it did not look planned—took a microphone, and instead of saying, "Thank you for coming, please buy my paintings," or even, "Hello," she began to wail. No band. No throng. (One or two dozen persons standing around looking at paintings were all that were there.) No evening gown or glittering jewels. No props. No backdrop. No fawning introduction by one of those people who do the fawning introductions to provide a buffer between a too-raw artist and an audience that has not yet decided where the context lies. Nothing between what was about to come out of her and the people who thought they were there to look at some paintings. At no risk of getting unevolved, unformulated emotion vomited all over their heads. There were no words Yoko formed. Just screams. Guttural. Sensual. Moan-y. Frightened. Frightening. Her fragile, nearly eighty-year-old body shook. She let loose something prehistoric, with all gusto. She was like a soldier with no army, no battle plan, launching into attack (or rescue), running forward all alone, no flanks, against an invisible enemy. Some people laughed. Some shuffled. She set down the mic and left, and people have been putting their comments about how they feel about it on YouTube ever since. Her performance is "pathetic," and she is "a moron" and a "cunt." And "why couldn't john killers [sic] shot her dumbass man that would have been perfect."

She doesn't respond to the hate. As a person, she is a letter-go. She says, "I'm a move-on girl." Not a stop-and-get-bothered girl. As an artist, Yoko Ono is a destroyer. A hole poker. A knock downer. Oh my, what big holes you have, grandmother. All the better to see through to what's already beautiful, my dear.

Her first film, in 1964, ambitiously titled *Film No. 1, a.k.a. A Walk to Taj Mahal*, was just that—the camera moved through a snowstorm. For an hour. No character development. No characters at all! No dialogue. Just snow. Because there is no person to see, *you* become the person; you are out in the snow, going you don't know where. There are no markers. Maybe it feels like static electricity, feels like water freezing, feels like untuned radio. Except there is no soundtrack. The audience is instructed to slowly pick apart white flowers, to provide their own soundtrack. Really, they're providing their own movie. Have you ever walked in the snow for a whole hour? You'd get so cold. Cold would be everything to you. But watching a movie of it, you're not cold. So if you experience something that is nothing but coldness, but it's not cold, is that nothing? What would come up, in an hour-long bed of nothing? What memories, ideas, desires? I am afraid of what would come out of deep in me! Are you?

Expanding your mind is a joke to people now—hippie claptrap. But it's a lot older than the 1960s. To ask disciples to do what cannot be done has been the path to enlightenment and broadening achievement in everything from architecture to love to leadership for thousands of years.

It's good for the state, for mass production, for us to be automatons, but it's not good for the human. Of what worth is your spirit and unique mind to you if not to understand what you've been brainwashed to accept as just the way it is. "Who are you to question God?" my grandmother would say, and threaten me with hell. "Who are you to question my authority?" my parent would say, and knock me down. Who am I? I'm the only me who *can* question where I, uniquely, landed. But how can I know what to ask, how to ask, when there is no training in my culture concerning questioning?

There is a long tradition in most cultures of exactly that. Koans. Riddles. Nonsense. The old wise man living in a cave, or wandering as a guest in the world, sometimes saying barely anything, eating barely anything except maybe some magic mushrooms, owning practically nothing. Most cultures call them mystics, and value their unusual and unbound outlooks, and when there was a question in your heart, you could climb up and be with them, on their mountain, and you were glad they were there. In America, they call themselves conspiracy theorists, and tend to get locked up in one institution or another. Others call them bums, and tell them to get a job. As if there is no value at all in building philosophies that don't fit into the system we have now, or just tearing down some old concepts to make room for a new arrangement of civilization that we haven't tried yet. Ono's work met the same reaction. Actually, so did her very existence.

For people with questions in their hearts, Yoko's conundrums can get us off of fixating on that question, and, distracted by her unanswerable question from going down our usual thought path, we find by surprise our answer down a side street. For example, by Yoko recording silence, we are in the position, should we take it, of figuring out what is silence. We assume silence is the absence of sound, thus the critics' fury over Ono selling an album that included recorded nothing.

That's spending your money and not getting something, right? Ono thinks nothing is something. She describes silence as "the sound of fear and darkness, like a child's fear that someone is behind him but he can't speak and communicate this." What do you think is the sound of silence? I'm sure your answer says something about you. And might be the answer to that question weighing on you.

You could listen to a million pop songs and not ever get to any of that. In fact, those million pop songs are part of what is keeping you from finding out what is truly there.

Forty-three years after Yoko Ono's film of snow and thirty-eight years after her track of no music, in 2007, in Iceland, she founded Imagine Peace Tower, which projects a beam of light. That's all it is. Light. Light is even less something than is snow, and twice as silent. She *made* this? What is it?!

Is light even allowed as a building material? How about dark? "Bagism" is when two people crawl into a bag so you can't see them, can't see what outfit or haircut or jewelry they're wearing, what role they're in, or if it's even "them" at all—who you thought it would be. This is to facilitate "total communication," where it would just be about what you're all saying, free from category. The people inside the bag can't see each other either, but just in case, they usually take their clothes off once they're in there. And then, commented John Lennon, who engaged in bagism with Yoko, people assumed they were "doing it"—but they never were. More "not"!

She introduced or helped along a lot of wacky ideas, like primal scream therapy. She and John Lennon brought onto the *Mike Douglas Show* this biorhythm feedback device where you put on a headband and attach wires to a keyboard and play it with your brain. All these ideas that were way out there, and maybe none of them got incorporated into popular culture, but often just provoked people to try something new, think something new—and though that might not lead directly to anything in and of itself, who knows what innovation in some other area reality-stretching might lead to? Leading indirectly is not much valued in our culture, because it is not quantifiable. And we do like our quantifying. We are a nation of accountants. What is your net worth?

It takes someone so lonely and outside anything of meaning to the rest of us to understand and communicate that we don't have to follow the rules. Nothing bad will happen. Yoko does not add. She takes away what is in the way. She lets go. She shows us that we could take away, too. Take away the order. Take away the clothes. Take away the roles. Take away the authority of one person over another. Take away the hierarchy. Take away the finish on the product. Take away the product. Take John out of his Beatles cage. Unlearn all you've learned. Take away everything you've been looking at, listening to, feeling, believing. Now what is left? What do you see when you turn off the TV, burn the canvases? What do you hear when you put the iPod in a drawer? What is left of the mother-child relationship when you don't accept the parts of it that society—neighbors, experts, reality shows—dictates but in which you don't believe? Or the wife-husband relationship? What if all that we thought of as "just how things are" turned out to have been barriers between us and the whole, wide world?

There are two schools of art. One is what is made beautiful by the artist; the other is to make way for the viewer to see or feel what is already beautiful. The first is to make something ornate and unreachably special with skills. The viewer or listener is awed, their belief regarding the order of things is confirmed, and they are reminded by this unachievable beauty of their own powerlessness. And I do love that kind of art, the beautiful kind. The other way to make art is to tear down what's between us and nature, us and eternity, us and the realization that everything is already perfect, everything. The viewer or listener loses respect for the current order or arrangement of civilization and becomes powerful, like King Kong, outside of civilization, like God, like the shuffling janitor who is pleased with his own good work and sleeps well.

I always admired the Japanese use of negative space in decorating and the unspoken in conversations (or so I gather from old films). Ono uses the negative positively. She is a classically trained operatic student who uses silence or screeches in her singing, a getter of coveted gallery showings who hangs unpainted canvases with requests for you to pound holes in them or walk on them. This first ever female admitted to an all-male philosophy university, who could travel the world discoursing multisyllabically all the way, tries lying in bed and not lifting a finger to cure the war. It takes an enormous lack of ego to not put your imprint on everything you do, to not employ your learning and position. To stand back, to hold back, to keep your mouth shut. To yell with your silence, a protest, when you know you very well could make soothing and welcomed sounds at the drop of a hat. She *could* sing; she knew how. And being a Beatles wife could have been a magic charm—but she wasn't interested. It takes all your willpower to overpower the will to power. To be accepted, to be thought nice, is Woman's power. That is something Yoko doesn't need.

She uses nonexistence in art and absence in her private life. Her first husband was composer Toshi Ichiyanagi. They grew apart, had an open marriage, then flew apart. Second husband, musician and promoter Tony Cox, same thing. Only he took her daughter, Kyoko, with him, and hid her from her mother in a religious cult. At first Yoko allowed third husband John Lennon to do what came naturally to him: to hunt for the lost daughter through private detectives and the courts. Only after John's death, when Yoko wrote an open letter to her now grown daughter, saying how deeply she loved Kyoko, but "you should not feel guilty if you choose not to reach me," and that she—Yoko—would no longer try to locate Kyoko, did her daughter slowly come back into her life. It's paradoxical, but it seems that when you accept loss, it loses its tenacity to stay lost. Yoko wived by letting husbands go; she mothered her daughter by letting her go. John Lennon got the urge to roam, and she said, "Go! Go roam!" And he did, and then he called and said, "I want to come home," and she said, "No, you're not ready." Yoko believes in the right to drift. She didn't want to hold down and lay claim on human beings any more than she did her art and ideas. It's all flow.

Everything that has happened to Yoko has caused her to get better and better at living on the outside (instead of trying to get in). She is out there in the lonely wide open—from being a silenced daughter to a war transplant to an expatriate to an unpopular artist to a feminist with no female friends to a lover blamed by the world for the breakup of their favorite band to losing her daughter to a cult to losing her husband to a killer. She manages all these losses and holds her ground, is not swept away. She is out there in nowhere or everywhere, and she tries to find beauty and she tries to find connection and she knows the pain of loneliness that is in all of us even though we might not be aware of it. But she is aware, and she reaches to that place in us, she wants us to know it's okay. We will be okay. Everything is all right.

Ono has made a career and a life out of doing exactly what she was not supposed to do, and not being what she was supposed to be. And when she does tell us what to do, it's the undoable. Because if you cannot do that, what else might you not do? The possibilities of the impossible are endless! Let banking and engineering deal with the doable, the possible. They build our houses and put food on our tables. But if we have no impossible as well, it's all rectangles and calories and dreamless sleep.

So... if I love her so much, why does this little old lady still make me so uncomfortable?

I am a huge Yoko Ono fan. I feel that what she does in art—tries to free people—is the most important thing you can do in life, period. And I love that she always does it, bravely, no matter who or what it goes against, no matter how much farther her unusual and uncompromising methods might drive her from our bosoms. Even now, at the most acceptable point her career or private life has ever reached in our moralistic and artistically anorexic society, who is embracing her? Courtney Love and Lady Gaga. And those women are nuts. They're extreme. We all love to watch what Love and Gaga do next, but who *likes* them? And while they catfight then make up and champion or co-opt other famous ladies, I never get the feeling *they* like *anyone*. It's more like the lonely and the aggressive recognizing each other, and choosing not to expend their energy trying to destroy each other. Maybe I watch too many Godzilla movies.

Back to Ono. I feel such intense appreciation for her, yet it is not a warm feeling. At some level I just don't understand her. It would please me so much if I could—it fills me with suppressed wariness that I don't. I don't judge anyone, yet I judge her. How could she sell John Lennon socks and ties with Kmart? Doesn't she have enough money? Sure, she keeps her *own* stuff uncommercialized, but what has she done to her late husband's? How could she cut poor Julian Lennon out of his inheritance when he'd already been abandoned by his father in life; why make him abandoned in his father's death as well? Why is she so wonderful in disinterested ways—communicating love to people she's never met, paving a hard path to peace inside and out for the loneliest of the loneliest among us—yet sometimes so *mean* in a personal way? I care about her. She puzzles me. There are areas where I wish she made different decisions, and it bothers me, but still I'm rooting for her. Then it bothers me that she bothers me; there's something wrong in me in that equation.

And that is how writing this little book caused me to question what I thought I knew of myself more deeply than at any time since probably my teenage years. How feminist am I if I have these questions about Yoko Ono but not about William S. Burroughs? He was so much more wretched a human being than she could ever be.

Female artists at the end of the day have to be somehow accessible. Yoko's not accessible. Just when you think you understand her feelings on things, like when she put John Lennon's smashed glasses on her album cover, you feel her vulnerability, you soften, then suddenly you find out she's been selling replicas of his murder clothes and pocketing the money and maybe shacking up with a businessman the whole time and there's a cover-up! Then you feel guilty that you were intrusive about how a widow mourns or how an artist alchemizes pain. And you step back, abashed, and you're back to square one: She's not accessible. Not figure-out-able. She *is* so weird. She's not endearing. Then again, she's not trying to be.

So what's wrong with the fact that I can't relate to her? I don't relate to male artists, or expect them to be my friends. It's about the work. I don't need to examine the human being in order to admire what they created. Which is lucky, because men don't seem to let that—whether I imagine I would like them as people or not—get in the way of their work.

But women do let it get in the way. When I need to work, I will attend instead to my kids' happiness, to my physical attractiveness, to my man's masculinity that seems like it could get bruised were I to let him see my ability to not see him or anyone or anything when I'm hot—or cold—on the pursuit of an idea, and I have this half-formed fear that he would find someone else who would better hide herself, or who maybe doesn't have so much to hide. I suspect other women of fitting better than I do inside this idea we have, or I have, of what a woman is, or a mother, or a lover, or a good person.

After all the decades of feminism, how can I still have such a problem with how much I can care about my work when there's even one person on my radar who needs something. It's stupid, I know, but knowing that just makes me hide it more strenuously, and make excuses for it. For having taken inside myself at last these patriarchal ideas of what a woman is, that I still don't believe, but out of fear that it might be true anyway, I live as if it were. Like a Catholic gone atheist will still secretly live a superstitious life just in case there is that hell he adamantly doesn't believe in, I let get in the way of communicating the truth making dinner, or how what I want to say would look like to a judge in a custody battle.

It wasn't always this way. I used to get so caught up in an idea I'd doggedly pursue it for days on end, to the neglect of loved ones and hygiene and anyone's expectations—including, but not limited to, the whole world. Many tried to squash down my not-fitting spirit, but I deflected it all, until my husband and I, both artists, had a contested, five-year-long divorce. My stuff was a little more undigestible or unexplainable than his, and he submitted to the court any shocking or sexual or politically unusual thing I'd ever written or performed in order to prove I was an unfit mother. The thought of showing *his* scandalous work in return to prove him an unfit father never occurred to me or to my attorney. Men are allowed to express all kinds of things and it is not thought of as impacting their ability to provide as fathers. Women, though—*everything* they think and do and are proves their worth or danger as mothers and wives. There's this underlying message about the need for purity and selflessness that you can avoid and avoid and avoid, and then, bam! One day you just stop being able to deflect, and you swallow it down, and it becomes you. But not with Yoko. "Mothers are not supposed to give guidance," she said, believing instead that children should do their own thing. I don't think I've ever heard anyone before proposing mothers should *not* guide their children. How different. How refreshing. And Yoko's had to deal with kidnapping, deportation, assassination—so much more spirit-breaking than my one custody battle, yet she absorbs it all and still says what she believes is true, not what will make her look like a good woman to the authorities.

This is why Yoko Ono is the ultimate feminist. She isn't fighting for women's rights per se, but she expresses herself doggedly and with a single-minded purpose of art for art's sake, truth for truth's sake, and doesn't seem to care what anyone thinks about her as a woman. Just like male artists do and we don't think anything of it. She's an *artist*, not a *woman artist*. Her life—and those of the people around her—is a tool. She uses incredibly personal autobiographical details in her work, yet she doesn't seem to feel any need for perfect factual order, or to worry about anyone's feelings. That quality is neither feminine nor masculine. It's genius, which is always disturbing when peered at too closely, but more so when it's housed in the body of a female, who should be maternal, who is supposed to be fuckable, agreeable, likable.

That is the ultimate feminism: Yoko Ono doesn't need us to like her. She doesn't care.

Then sometimes I think she does care.

Oh, Yoko Ono, you trouble me so.

SOME PIECES

From her 1964 book *Grapefruit* comes the instruction *Stone Piece*: "Take the sound of the stone again."

Wall Piece is the audience members and Yoko all bashing their heads against the wall.

Yoko used a stethoscope to listen to a clock.

She wrapped lion statues in Trafalgar Square in brown paper. No one cared. I wonder what that was supposed to mean. If anything.

THERE WERE FIGHTS

Anything unsortable is threatening, and Yoko is unidentifiable. People want to know what they are dealing with. There is a strong human need to categorize. Yoko is unknowable. No one really relates to her. She stimulates what's already there but had been background, buried, ignorable. She does not show; she does not give us something with which to cover any blankness that may be lurking. She's in the way, and way out there. Everyone needs to feel like they have an answer, but there is no explanation for Yoko Ono. She's a catalyst, but it's all about you. Yoko gives us nothing, she tries to show us what we already have. In some cases, that might be close to nothing, and to edge closer to that realization could make a person uncomfortable to the point of hostility.

Yoko comes from a long line of the unquantifiable. In 805, Yoko's ancestor Saicho recently returned from a two-year visit to China, created a new Buddhist sect, Tendai Lotus, which mixed Chinese traditions with Japanese: theory, debate, calligraphy, and the esoteric as paths to enlightenment. Plus, he introduced tea to Japan.

There were fights. Saicho was condemned as transgressive. It was said that he didn't keep private stuff for monks private, but went around making enlightenment secrets available to any old body.

Yoko's great-grandfather Atsushi Saisho, a "luminary" to the emperor, had the gall to let white people onto a chain of Japanese islands where they had never been before. Always mixing it up, this clan! Atsushi Saisho had no sons, only a daughter, which was supposed to be a shameful thing, but he didn't care, he was proud of her. She was Yoko's grandmother Tsuruko, and she studied English and music at college in the 1800s, which was unusual for a woman.

In 1952, Yoko was the first ever woman to major in philosophy at Japan's Gakushuin University. But once she'd broken in and was accepted, she didn't want it anymore, and a year later left, for America. Impermanence. We are all water.

PRETTY

Born in Tokyo in 1933 to a banker family, Yoko was a rich little girl left alone, to be brought out as a showpiece in front of company. She was a quiet girl, keeping to herself, and her mother told her she was not pretty. She was considered handsome. Which is okay. But if your only value is as a showpiece, and you're not a pretty piece to show... God, how alone must you feel in the world? Her mother was very pretty.

The familial line was made of rebels, but Yoko's parents decided to tamp down the rebellion in themselves and expected the same of their firstborn. Yoko practically had no father—he was away most of her life; she had only her mother. Despite the lady living there in the same house, Yoko was rather unmothered as well.

Yoko quietly questioned and bucked against what was expected of her as a little girl, as a daughter, the same way she later questioned and bucked against what she was supposed to be as a mother, as a wife, as a lover, as an artist. The not-pretty little girl grew up to be a not-pretty little woman. She was culturally important and influential and smart and loving and brave. Yet still her degree of prettiness is how she is judged. Even now. On YouTube, a user calling himself Roger Rod typed the comment, "Anybody that ever questions the destructive effect upon that brain that results from drug abuse, John thought Yoko was beautiful."

DESPAIR AND LONELINESS, OR, WHAT IT FELT LIKE TO BE AN ASIAN WOMAN TRYING TO MAKE ART AND MAKE HER WAY IN AMERICA, 1960

*B**lood Piece* says to paint with your blood. "Keep painting until you die." Not paint to live. Not paint to keep. Out, out, out, get it out.

That is despair.

Blood Piece was created in the spring of 1960. Yoko was living in a cold-water flat in Tribeca, in New York, in a marriage (to a fellow Japanese) with all the love gone out of it, and no money. She spent her time passionately doing art that was supposed to change the world, but no one much cared.

In April of 1960, Woolworth's lunch counter was still segregated, the Civil Rights Act had not yet been signed, and the birth control pill had not yet been approved.

In 1960, Norman Rockwell completed *Triple Self-Portrait*. You could buy a print of it today for $90.99 at Kohl's. *Blood Piece* is not listed for sale anywhere.

In 1962, Yoko Ono got committed to a mental institution.

FLUXUS

Fluxus was an international group of practitioners of the absurd based in New York City in the '60s. They organized art shows, experimental performances of music, dance, theater....

In 1960, before Fluxus was Fluxus, La Monte Young had been using Ono's Tribeca loft, where she was already burning her own paintings, for Happenings. John Cage told her to put fire retardant on them, luckily, or her lesson in impermanence could have become one of permanence, the people being literally transformed to ash instead of their minds opened by the burning.

She hung out with these men, yes—who wouldn't? She learned from them. They learned from her, too. She slept with some of them. But she never joined them. Her life was enough; she did not need a movement. Born in 1933. Tokyo firebombing in 1945. Burn her own work in 1960. That's enough.

She would work with anyone, but she always stayed Yoko; she would become one of nobody, no group or movement. Still, she was just starting out in 1960, when Fluxus was just coalescing. You would think that would be when, if ever, a struggling artist, practically disowned by her parents, would latch onto an offered hand. Since Yoko is so ungossipy, it's hard to know exactly why she ultimately refused to join this loose bunch of like-minded conceptual artists, composers, musicians, performers, poets, but I suspect she thought they were too uptight about their looseness. Her friend George Maciunas gave it the name Fluxus a few years into the various performances the bunch of them had been doing, and maybe just that made it too stiff a thing for Yoko to let claim her as its own: that it had a name.

Maybe she didn't join Fluxus because she is just incapable of joining anything. She lived two blocks from Andy Warhol. Everyone else was hurling themselves into his Factory movies and lifestyle, and she did compose music for one of his short films (*Love*), but she kept her distance. She was interested in him, but not in crawling under his umbrella.

Fluxus seemed to me a second-rate Dada. Dadaists were funny. They were distraught about the war, the Great War, which started in 1914. Dada was born in 1916. It wasn't really planned-out lessons for opening people's minds. No one knew they were attending a Happening. The audience didn't know they were an audience. They thought they were going to dinner; then Tristan Tzara stood on the table and began to recite. Dadaists were drunk and sarcastic and hurt by the cruelty they'd witnessed, and expressed what was hysterical by being hysterical: with gibberish and nonsense, cut-up newspapers, and people painted into disjointed planes. Of course they were real artists at the same time, real poets, real workers. But they felt life as stabbing them, as trapping them, and they'd seen what it had done to other people through greed, through hypnotizing people. They'd seen terrible cruelty, not only perpetrated, but allowed, even celebrated en masse as patriotic. Dada was a bunch of crazy people clapping their hands and yelling in the faces of the other people who were still asleep and didn't know it. And didn't know something terrible was happening to their bodies, to their minds, to the earth, while they slept.

Fluxus came out of Dada, but was just a little late and a little cold of a movement for my taste. Yoko may be a little chilly in some ways, but there's also something wonderfully haphazard and frustrating about her that the more carefully constructed or thought-out Fluxus Happenings lacked. They were too studied or purposeful to amuse, startle, wake up a sleeping world. It was like they'd come to the conclusion or results they wanted before they started a project, and they'd direct the audience thusly. I don't think Yoko ever knew what would or should happen. "Every time I turn around, there's a big surprise," she said in an interview. And there was a desperate need or search for kindness in Yoko's pieces. Like mailing seeds to world leaders so they could grow trees. That's so naïve. It takes balls to pursue a gentle dream, in the face of all you know, and Yoko knew a lot.

Dada, and Yoko, seem to me reaction first, and then they'd— or you would—find the concept from there. Fluxus seems to me concept first, and then trying to manufacture the reaction that should come out of that idea. I think Yoko had a distance between what she felt and knew and saw and what came out of her. "What I'm trying to do is make something happen by throwing a pebble into the water and creating ripples. . . . I don't want to control the ripples." I think sometimes it was concept first—like with all of her instructions where she had no idea how they would be carried out—and sometimes it was reaction first, like when she'd emit prehistoric guttural sounds rather than repeating pre-chosen rhyming words. But either way, the distance between reaction and concept was great in her. It seems like there's so much distance in her. Always reaching across. Always too wide to reach.

She said she never knew what the reaction to her events or pieces or music would be. It seemed like Fluxus collectively knew, or decided, what the reaction *should* be.

DEVIL'S ADVOCATE...
EXCEPT SHE'D
PROBABLY ARGUE
WITH HIM, TOO

She wore black when everyone else wore colors. When other houses were wood and greens and embroidery pillows, she made hers all white. After social protests and before No Wave (the angry and unmelodious musicians and filmmaking youth who wore black and were in black moods in late-1970s New York—Lydia Lunch, James Chance, Nick Zedd), she said yes. On that tiny placard, in tiny type, on the ceiling that you had to climb a ladder to read: "Yes!" When American pop culture was finally able to find this weird and dark and tiny foreigner fuckable, she sang: *No, no, no.* When women wore flowers in their hair, she sang: *I'm a witch; I'm a bitch.* When people finally got used to her and her subjects being naked in our faces, she invented bagism. It's about being invisible, so as to finally be visible.

BURNING

Yoko Ono wrote, "Burn this book," in her first published book, *Grapefruit*, 1964, six years before Abbie Hoffman wrote *Steal This Book*.

Previously, book burning was a negative, about suppression. Think Ray Bradbury's *Fahrenheit 451*. Or that crazy emperor Qin Shi Huang ordering all intellectual and philosophical books burned in 213 B.C. Or uptight mothers banding together and demanding—and getting—books or music that might lead to something blamed and burned, broken, banned. Yoko loves creation, but not so much preservation. She loves, too, destruction, for what it opens up. As when she called herself a nigger, she turned the fire into a cleansing. When the old, sturdy trees are razed, the tender seedlings get some sun.

Read this book. Burn your life.

CUT

In 1964, a young, striking unknown artist sat down on a stage in Tokyo and invited the audience to come up to her with scissors and cut off a piece of her clothing. The invitation, or instruction, was just one printed word; nothing was said. On the paper was written: "Cut." The girl stared straight ahead. They could have stabbed her. She was so brave, so implacable and resolute and easily wounded and tender. Look at her face, her skin, when she sits silent and small, and they come at her one after another, these people in beehives and business suits, and they cut and cut. One man cuts her bra, and her eyes roll uncontrollably. She's frightened.

How often are women and girls looked at in a threatening, cutting-off-clothes way, just as a normal part of the day?

In Tokyo, the cutters were shy. When Ono performed the piece in London some months later, there the cutters were violent. Is it differing natures of differing societies, or do strangers treat an exposed and helpless person who looks like them and their family better than an exposed and helpless person who looks different from them and their family? I think Ono thought disrobing would remove some apparent differences, show the sameness that's underneath. I guess she didn't realize how deep racism goes. Or she did know, and wanted to show it, demonstrate it to people using their own hands, their own actions.

In *Cut*, she has made the audience the artist, herself the canvas to do with what they would, the screen on which to project the movie of the reality inside them—would they cut off her underwear? Would they cut off her hair, her fingernails, her eyelashes? Women expose themselves and show nothing of their true feelings every day, every night, in strip clubs, in porn, in modeling, in unhappy marriages, in desperate bars, with popular potential boyfriends, with the fear of displeasing when walking down the street wearing tight, short dresses.

Yoko was turning inside out the sad, stunned silence inside women, hidden even from themselves, hidden beneath our raucous laughter when hooted at and our exclamations of pleasure when gifted with slut heels and leopard miniskirts and our grinding walk and yelling back at the yellers, catcallers.

Two years before the first performance, in 1962, Yoko wrote for *Grapefruit* an instruction called *Cut Piece*. It said: "Throw it off a high building." That was the whole thing. Throw what? I don't know. It's a feeling, I think. Throw it off a high building is a feeling I have sometimes. It's violent and calm and peaceful at the same time. It's an end in a beginning. It's the satisfaction of knowing you have nothing to lose because you just threw over the last thing you were holding onto, the last thing that could have been taken from you. And now all that's left is just your life, just the living. It's whole, it's one, it can't be chipped off and away, this thing that's left of you after you threw off a high building all that could be thrown.

In 2003, Ono did *Cut* again, in Paris this time. Matronly body, a beloved icon, old. The mood was different. Yoko said she did it with love rather than with the "anger and turbulence" she felt in 1964. She wanted people to take from her now, and the taking didn't make her lose. Like when somebody lies in the shade of a tree, peels a piece of bark off to play with... No harm done. She didn't have to give of herself. She was famous by then. She was rich. She could buy whatever she wanted. No need to barter herself for free drinks or rent paid or money for school. Her career was set, her future stability ensured; nothing to sacrifice for, to build toward. She was on that stage inviting people to cut off her clothes as a seventy-year-old because she wanted to give herself. One of the audience members invited to cut was her son, Sean Lennon, twenty-seven years old at the time.

It felt different from the outside as well. In our society, what she did in the young *Cut* is no odder than what a really lazy stripper does on a bad night. Why do we think of old ladies as vulnerable, but sexy young things as provocative, asking for it? I suppose the difference is we want to see young girls naked, and we really don't want to know what goes on in an old body. It looks scary. It forces us to confront mortality. But why do we ascribe our own desires or repulsions to the object, as if they emanate from the object... the smooth, ripe girl... as if she did this to us, put this feeling in us, and now she deserves the way we feel toward her and how we act on those feelings toward her.

Watching the video of people lining up in 2003 to cut holes out of the clothes of this straight-backed, bespectacled septuagenarian, her big bra still on, I thought, "Where would I cut?" Her face and limbs were impassive; I could have snipped a bra strap and let one of those big, saggy, old-lady bosoms fall down—how embarrassing. But it would be me who was embarrassed, to do that, to think of an appropriately aging body, breasts that gave milk to children and pleasure to lovers, as a chance to humiliate. It would be me who had something wrong, not the breast that has not been operated on and exercised and Spanxed into a cartoon of what female is. Being female means making you want it, right?

Ono turned being violently or greedily exposed by the world into a wonderful exposing of self by self to the world. She said she felt vulnerable after the World Trade Center attacks on 9/11. She felt the need for people to trust each other again. She was willing to go first. She offered herself, her frail body, in a compromising position, having faith that these two hundred strangers (and her son) would be peaceful and kind. And they were. An eighteen-year-old cutter, Katherine Williams, said: "Scissors usually have a violent connotation, but [Yoko] turns it around to make it peaceful. You can make peace out of violence."

Both in 1964 and in 2003, when she was stripped of her black clothing—the artist's uniform—what authority would she have left? She allowed the audience to become the artist by letting them make the art... make the cuts that made her new image. By Ono's allowing her recognizability as the artist to be removed, there still had to be *some* artist there—this was an art piece, after all. Imagine if the CEO wanted his workers to stop being automatons and start caring about the direction and viability of the company, and he allowed the staff to rise up and each cut off one piece of his thousand-dollar suit until he was naked...burn the pieces with the lit tip of a cigar... dismantle his watch that contains mini-faces telling the time on three different continents. See him naked and wormy and helpless. He would be gambling that the vision would also turn topsy-turvy...staff would realize they are managers all, and start running this company with gusto and confidence. In life, in art, in relationships, there are the managers and the managed. Creators and consumers. Controllers and controlled. I suppose there needs to be organization for things to run smoothly. I don't think things running smoothly is Yoko's goal.

"But business is not like art," you say. "Business needs a pecking order, or nothing would get done. Like armies. Whereas art is done for love; the arts are about communication and equality." No, it isn't. The art world is all about who you know and the authority given to you by such and such a critic, or quote, or iconicized picture, or celebrity endorsement, or a smart move like getting shot or persecuted, for believability. There are bribes and prostitution and politics in the art world, too.

Or in the family. Imagine if the high-earning parent were to call in the children and the elderly relatives and the stay-at-home parent and ask them to cut to pieces his or her credit cards, power-saw his vehicle, strip the heels off his work shoes. What would happen inside the children, the homemaker, and the elderly, were the money supplier/rule maker divested of authority? I don't know. And Yoko could not have known either what would happen when she invited her audience to strip her, to take over making her paintings, to do her job, take her role, and destroy her authority.

"We're born in a prison, raised in a prison.../We dream in a prison like fools" (Plastic Ono Band, "Born in a Prison"). We can dream our way right out of that prison—our role, arrangement—too.

Interestingly, the original script for *Cut* says the performer, the one getting cut, does not have to be a woman.

BAG

Cut Piece is about taking off the uniform/role to reveal the pure human. *Bag Piece* is about covering over what covers up the pure human.

Yoko did her first *Bag Piece* performance by climbing into a black sack with then husband Tony Cox in Tokyo in 1964. Reaction: not much.

She and John called it "bagism" when John Lennon was her partner inside the sack at a press conference in Vienna in 1969. Reaction: John said the press pointed the mic at the bag and said, "What are you wearing in there?"

In 2003 in New York, Peter Jennings thought he was going to interview Yoko, but instead was dragged into the bag to become an unwitting participant in the exploration of finding the pure human. Reaction: The famous reporter was heard to say, "Help!" before emerging, panting, and hiding behind a support beam to adjust his interviewer self back into place.

TO LOSE IS TO SAVE

I went to see some famous belly dancers. Despite warnings over the loudspeakers not to photograph as it would distract the dancers, a sea of phones rose up all around me. I couldn't concentrate on what was happening on the stage because everyone was storing the experience in their lit-up boxes to control later, to start and stop at their command. It's greed. It's ownership. We make slaves of moments. We want to keep experiences, which is not at all the same as having them.

Lay a canvas out, let the moon paint it in light. Let the dawn paint it, too. Throw it in the garbage.

That's my favorite of her instructions in *Grapefruit*, especially the last line. If we throw the rendition away, we can't be reminded of another's vision of the thing, what colors they chose, how to crop it, or how to describe it. Where to focus; what to leave in, what to leave out. Except this wasn't even a rendition! It was us seeing moonlight on a canvas. And then, even though the canvas no longer holds the moonlight, stills throw it in the garbage so that we can never see it again, and never get confused that the canvas holds light, or rendering of light, or even our memory of the light that night. Light is its own thing. It exists. It doesn't have to be named and stored by specialists. Having more expensive equipment or schooling doesn't make them see any more light than you do, or any better light, which they can then charge us access to. Yoko's instruction forces us to hold the light in our memory, not holding how an artist or photographer or writer saw it externally, in a painting or photograph or book. This way we also keep us, the person we were, that night that we looked at the moonlight on the naked canvas. We have to understand it while it's there. That's the way you have a memory, when our external memory keepers are unplugged. To be extra sure you'll really be there, she makes sure even the thing you saw the moonlight on will be gone. The garbage will swallow the canvas the way the moon will be drowned by the sun.

She takes away the luxury of allowing the expert to translate beauty for us, and equipment to hold for us, moonlight or dawn's light, before we ever have a chance to see it in its own language or remember it instead of storing it externally, on some disk or memory card. To not be told what we're seeing, and to not have any screen to keep it for us to ponder later, means we have to know it ourselves, now. Which is the biblical word for loving, for respecting, for having sex with, for speaking directly to God.

Yoko was a young woman when she wrote that moonlight instruction, in the summer of 1961. The young are not usually concerned with preserving or remembering anything. Especially not in the summertime. Yoko had already lost so much, been losing this whole time, this whole life, that she had already learned the art, the necessity, of alchemizing losing into having.

She'll tell you to set something on fire to watch the smoke. What you see in the smoke makes the painting. That relies on chance, on you, on the elements. So impermanent!

In life, it seems to me, she holds onto the smoke and lets go of the thing set on fire. She keeps and uses the remains—

recorded fragments—of people, but is never intrusive with people themselves, never begging. She's a move-on girl.

She had to be. As a child, Yoko got everything taken from her by the war. Her father, her country, her position in society. As a woman, still she lost. It almost seems like it became an addiction, or it was just her nature to lose.

She had to learn how to like losing. Or maybe she liked seeing how it didn't break her. Perhaps her early losses kept her feeling like she didn't fit anywhere, like she was always about to lose, and when it didn't feel like that, it felt claustrophobic, so she started slipping out of places, relationships, identities, movements, to kick-start the inevitable loss. Or perhaps she was making sure *she* did not get lost inside of someone or something or somewhere.

No. It's not that she came to *like* losing. It's that she strengthened her ability to see energy as movement, and it's energy that matters, not where or in whom it's currently resting or at what point it's departing. You can't hog it. It won't be trapped; it won't stay still. It's not that she ever liked losing. It's that she became more able to perceive time as not separated into segments: past, present, and future, each beyond reach of the other segments of itself. She began seeing the connections rather than the segregation. And to see people not separated into bordered entities that must not be crossed: you, me, our kind, and Other. When you see the connections, when you see what is uninterrupted flowing through every living thing, there is no foreigner. There is no enemy. Not even death.

She lost baby after baby after baby. To abortion in her first marriage, to miscarriage in her third. I have lost fetuses. It's not the fetus you lose. It's not something the size of a fist to you, the mother. It is the child's whole future, which you felt and held warm inside, coiled and dewy until ready to be released, to unfold. You feel and see the child's future spreading out even into after you've died. You feel the child like a stone thrown into a river with nearly endless ripples. You already feel and know the ripples that have not yet ringed out, because the stone-size fetus has not yet been flung into his life. This is what you lose when you lose a baby. You lose the lifetime you already saw, which you were sworn to protect.

She took all the pain of all her losses, and she alchemized it into art and a philosophy of connectedness of everyone and everything already, so you didn't need to form or preserve any apparent connections, you could just become aware of what was already there. And you didn't have to experience loss as negative, because it goes somewhere; it's positive somewhere, and you're everywhere, so what leaves you comes back to you. You as other. Other as you. It's a matter of shifting your perspective.

She didn't want to keep the ability to transcend loss to herself. She told the world, in books and paintings and songs and dance and Happenings, and how to experience without possessing. The world said, "You're crazy." And, "You're boring." And, "Shut up."

The insults don't stop her anymore than the loss ever does, never even makes her have less life. She allows anything to be taken from her, and more rushes in to fill the vacuum. She does not try to block life from flowing from her, and so it so easily flows to her, through her. There's always more. There's plenty. Loss is only movement.

EARTHQUAKE BABY

In 2008, in New York City, Ono exhibited *Touch Me*, which included a life-size woman's body, lying down, made out of a mushy substance, and people could touch it. They poked it so roughly, especially around the nipples, genitals, mouth, and eyes, that they eroded holes out of it. She left it like that, feeling that that said something, visually, about how women experience being poked and probed and treated with forceful intrusion.

When she repeated the installation in Venice, Italy, in 2009, she decided to make the woman out of marble, wanting now to protect the woman's body, even though it was just an image. Why not show a woman as indestructible sometimes, instead of always pointing out the ruin? When you're truly always changing, you can't stay *always* changing, or that's staying the same. Visitors were invited to dip their fingers in a bowl of water and feel the woman's hard, smooth, unalterable body.

I'm not putting these sections in chronological, or really any, order. She doesn't live or work in order, never did, so how could I shove her into one? She loops. She re-looks. She doesn't quite finish anything. It's always alive that way. She said, "Don't call it progression. It's not a progression." That would require a plan. A plan means you predict reaction, result. Then you achieve it. Then it's achieved. Now the thing is identifiable. Idea, execution, executed. Next! Ono did not plan, did not have expectation for correct reaction or interpretation. She did not guide. She just did. "When I think of an idea, I go with it. I don't think twice."

She sends her ideas leaping across time and place, allowing them to interact with different eras and cultures and come out different every time. *Cut Piece* was written in 1962 as an instruction or a sort of koan, desperate; performed in 1964, angry; performed in 2003, with love. *Touch Me* in 2008 was woman's body destroyed. *Touch Me* in 2009 was woman preserved. In 2012 in India, Yoko is doing an exhibit called "Remember Us," with dismembered women's body parts preserved through memory (casts and ash). She made the film *Fly* in 1970, with a fly crawling across a naked woman, and the album *Fly* in 1970—an avant-garde looping synthesizers and buzzing vocals.

She composed unfinished scores. That means every time the piece is performed, it becomes what the performers feel and believe and know in that moment, and how they play off each other and the audience and what is happening on the streets, and what is happening in their home, their family, their culture, their heart. It will never be finished. It will never be gotten right. That's the terrain Yoko Ono rides.

In her personal life, too: She kept marrying musicians from different countries whom she shouldn't have for one reason or another—poor men, young men, already married men. Divorced when she shouldn't, costing her her relationship first with her parents, next with her daughter. With people, as with ideas, she goes with it, doesn't think twice. Why fear possible results? Why try to hold onto a situation? Why try for control or safety (predictability) when you know in your bones it will be taken away? No one can take it from you if you give it away first; put it down and walk away from it. You can do it again in another place with another person, and it will be a new mix, coming back to the same experience through another door, and it will be different and it will be the same. Reincarnation flowing through a life without any dying. Don't call it progression, because that makes it linear, that breaks things up: beginning, middle, and end. Instead, Yoko sees the eternal, which is only reapproached, which changes only according to which direction you're coming to it from.

By allowing for loss, not trying to stop it, even encouraging it, by incorporating loss as a stage that everything transforms into and out of, she reconceptualized what constitutes a relationship.

It's not just individual works of art that are touchable, unfinished, and finishable by you (anyone), but Yoko herself, as an artist. She was not constrained by definition of singer to sing, or sculptor to complete solid works, or artist as poor, or elderly as sedate—at eighty years old, she is sexy, cool, creative. She is not even bound to not being bound. At first she let everyone poke holes in her spongy woman; then she changed it, and protected the next body from touch's effects, breaking her own rule just like she breaks everybody else's.

YOKO SAID...

Nineteen sixties New York. Yoko was too hot-blooded for the cool and too cold for the warm-blooded. Yoko said, "Avant-garde boys didn't use the voice. They were all just so cool [and] asexual." While she "wanted to throw blood" with her voice.

Think of the Velvet Underground. No heavy lifting with that voice. They sing about wanting to "nullify my life," fall into the dream. Yoko wants to wake you up into your life. VU's Lou Reed matches Yoko in feeling like an outsider. Jewish, considered small and ugly, he, too was committed to a mental institution, and then committed himself for a while to a heroin lobotomy. But I think Yoko strives to express herself out of the hole she finds herself in, while Lou Reed was content to stay under the surface and find what is lovely down there, and make unusual overlaid melodies out of it, and find the perfect lines. I see young Lou Reed as a person left behind in pain, reaching for what's lovely, or trying to bury what is ugly under layers of lovely sounds and rhymes and getting it right. Yoko didn't do that. She didn't create. She unhooked the bindings. There is a need for both approaches. I just don't understand why he is so accepted and Yoko was laughed off. He's a great poet, but he didn't come back for us from the beyond. He just communicates so perfectly what he finds out there. *Metal Machine Music* may be the exception.

But even on that album, the blood flows through Lou Reed's fingers on his guitar angry and otherworldly and unfinished, but there will be no throwing of that blood. There is still something dispassionate about the creating of this music that is so full with passion. He is still the artist and we the listener, and that barrier has not been attacked.

Attacked is the word author/singer Barb Jungr used to describe what Yoko did to vocalizing in the early days.

Yoko was a conceptual artist who felt trapped in the ivory tower of conceptual art. She wanted something throbbing and sensual and real, something base, something witty, something dirty. But she was who she was—an actor in the fifth dimension of the not-yet-happened. She'd divorced the Japanese composer Ichiyanagi and married American musician/producer Cox, had a child, gotten a little fame. None of it really seemed to stick. If only something would *happen*, something irresistible. Something undeniable. Maybe funny and even sweet. And just a little grounding. What a relief that would be for our rocket woman.

THE $3000 APPLE

In the Indica Gallery in London in 1966, Yoko had an apple for sale for £200. That's US $3,000 in today's dollars. This is the apple John Lennon walked in and bit, when he didn't know Yoko Ono, and apparently he didn't see the price tag or didn't respect that this apple was an art piece.

John Lennon could buy anything—a pet monkey, a plane, a posse. When money is limitless, all things lose meaning—when they can't be dreamt of and saved for, and maybe not gotten. How refreshing it must have been to see value inverted. If what is free (to be plucked easily off trees seeming to line every path) can be made beyond the common man's ability to acquire, than what is beyond the common man's ability to acquire must be free. How amazing, this apple!

How nice for Yoko that someone would mistake her art piece for the real thing, and bite it. All of her art was turning the real thing into art pieces so people would put on their special important expensive viewing eyes and just maybe they would see it, what had been there all along. They could have seen the real thing all the time, everywhere, but forgot to.

All Yoko Ono ever wanted was for people to bite what they thought could not be bitten, see what they thought could not be seen, know what they thought could not be known.

She was, it seems, Satan.

But there was a mistake in telling the story. Satan was the good guy. God didn't want us to bite the apple of knowledge because then we'd know we were Him, and the patriarchy, the whole order of things, would turn to dust.

YOKO AND THE BLUES

Anyway, John bit that apple, and she yelled at him. I think it was very exciting for him to be chastised, because nobody else was chastising him. They didn't dare. Can you imagine how lonely it must be to be at the top of your craft, at the top of the world, with everybody agreeing with anything you say and nobody having anything to offer about how to live, how to create, how to move on? How lost must one be up there. Women were cloying. Men let him do his thing. Who could teach John Lennon about how to write a great song? Nobody. Yoko taught him how to unwrite. How to do something else entirely, and make that a song. She expanded what a song is, what a song means, for John Lennon. A song is silence. A song is moans. A song is feedback. A song is a wail. Of course he knew a lot of that from old blues tracks, but he'd forgotten. And she taught him what life is like for nonwhite nonmales. This, too, you get from the blues. But Yoko may have been more... insistent.

And she was eager to absorb him, to learn from him, to trade essences. She'd gone so far out for so long, and she wanted to come down, come in. He could take her in. She said, "When John and I got together, I was interested in [rock]—that strong, heavy beat, which I equated with the heartbeat. I thought avant-garde music is mainly for the head." She was interested now in regions below.

He was tired of being a pop superstar and she was disillusioned with the ivory tower of the avant-garde...the elitism...the inability of mere mortals to understand such an elevated movement. And the avant-garde were becoming disillusioned with her. Her films and art were becoming too possible to see, too written about. The avant-garde did not consider themselves of the people, but rather above the people, needing to lead the silly and the blind. All Yoko wanted was what was real, what was people. A true artist is about what is true, not about what is art. A true artist is looking in on the people, trying forever to get in, to get to them, to be with them, of them. Yoko's living in her head too much and hanging around exclusively "special" people had distanced her. John was a down-to-earth, humorous guy, but the fame and the blinding awe with which he was received had distanced him. In each other, the pair found gravity.

And so John and Yoko slowly traded mantles. She took on rhymes and melody and he descended into a pretalent, unquantified state. Talent can be a disguise, pleasantness a cover-upper. John's vocals after Yoko—some of it was barking, grunting, screaming. Something inside, a longing, a fury, a need, that had been buried all those years under an avalanche of sounds that made sense, a voice that made people happy, a guitar that went along, that made heads nod and the sun come out...Yoko saw that buried thing in John and said, "Come out, I see you," and out that buried thing came, blinking. This stunted, ugly creature who had been there all along, the one who got left, who got hidden, came out howling, and said, "I *am* here. You fuckers. I'm alive. You didn't kill me, or erase me, and I didn't kill me either, when I was trying so hard to be someone else to make you happy."

John Lennon's "Mother" (1970) is so much more raw and inwardly exploratory and daring than songs by the Beatles ever were. It was time for a change. Cannibalism is necessary in music, but please, not of your own band.

To an abused and abandoned child all grown up, "Mother" provides a soundtrack to what your mouth and hands were sealed off from expressing during those silenced formative years. "I Want to Hold Your Hand" is a very nice song, but to some people, very nice doesn't mean much.

And for Yoko, suddenly the new-to-her "nice" *did* mean something to the formerly austere, grim, formal foreigner. John made her laugh and feel safe. The security and faith and jokes John gave to Yoko freed her from having to express ugliness and pain and aloneness so nonstop; she didn't have to always be trying to exorcise it...because sometimes it wasn't there anymore. She was able to experiment with, to brush up against, what is pretty, what pleases.

NAIL

Okay, it turns out I mixed up how they met. There was an imaginary nail first, *then* the apple got bit. But since Yoko always mixes it up, I felt like I should leave it that way. Here's another order:

The gallery owner, John Dunbar, had brought John Lennon there the night before Yoko's opening. Lennon was king; he went where he wanted when he wanted and got what he wanted. Yoko was running around making sure everything was ready for the next day. She didn't know who Lennon or the Beatles were, or if she knew, she didn't care. She was famous enough in her own circle, and she didn't even like or care about her own little fame; why would she care about someone else's? One of her paintings was a canvas with the instruction to hammer a nail into it. Lennon picked up a nail and the hammer, and she rushed over and said, "You can't do that; the exhibition hasn't opened." John Dunbar came over and said, "Yoko, John is a billionaire. Artists need patrons!" Yoko said to Lennon, "For five shillings, you can pound a nail in." Lennon, who was so rich and popular and pampered he never carried cash, said, "I haven't any money. How about if I give you five imaginary shillings to pound in an imaginary nail?" She thought that was funny, but he was eager for more banter, and she was busy, so she handed him an instruction, meant to send him on his way. It said: "Breathe." So he panted like a dog, and did not leave, and waited for more. And when she finally convinced him to go, he bit the apple on his way out. He wanted more. More of that nothing she was so prolific in. Nothing is so refreshing.

I think what she meant by the instruction "Breathe" was probably: Don't worry where or when "it" is—the time to pound nails into the canvas, or the time to touch me. Right now is now, and when it's the right time or place for something else, then that will be right now, right here. Breathe. That's life, going in and out of your throat. It will be the same when what you're waiting for arrives. It's all life. You are where it's at, baby!

And he answered, with dog-panting, like a little kid, a funny kid, playful, which I imagine is the ultimate enlightened stage. She gave him gravity and depth; he gave her ease and rising up, light laughing.

He was married, with a child; she was married, with a child.

She'd do things with other famous artists, like Andy Warhol, Ornette Coleman, but not align herself long enough to get swallowed. With Lennon it was the same at first. He sponsored one of her exhibitions, they hung out, she'd mail him instructions—like, "Go to an imaginary lighthouse." Then, when he was getting too pant-y, she disengaged, took off for Paris for political insurrection.

Beatles fans and the press's hateful reaction to her came from fear of a man-woman union. In the 1960s, men and women complemented each other in their separate roles. It was still a carryover from a century earlier when the West was still (or more rabidly) God-fearing, yet we had the industrial revolution, capitalism, free market, stock market, factories, moving from the country to the city, and business became how one earned a living, not creating food and useful items with your family, and bartering and being neighborly. Making money became how one made money, and it was a dirty business. Yet everyone believed in heaven still, and wanted to get in, but how were they going to get in when they'd been dishonest and exploitative every day at work? The answer came in separation of roles for men and women. Women stayed home and stayed pure—meaning dumb. They didn't dirty their hands in plunder; they didn't make back-alley deals. They raised children, dusted, made dinner, embroidered, and didn't even have dirty thoughts, much less dirty deeds. They were like big children, and God never bars children from heaven. So the deal became when you married, your souls combined, and on Judgment Day, you both would be let in if her soul was white (unknowing of sin) enough to balance your black one down to a pale gray. So men really had to deceive their wives about the cheating things they did, if they didn't want to plunge both of the marrieds into the everlasting hellfire! This ideology or superstition took powerful hold, and was still in effect even after women began to trickle into the workplace and even after atheists began coming out of the woodwork. Even today, it lingers just below our conscious thought. I've had boyfriends who were drug dealers and boyfriends in banking and finance. In both cases, they said to me about their workday, "The less you know, the better." Do you think they'd be saying that to me if they were women and I a man? And what is it the girlfriend is supposed to hide from the man? Her impurities. Her past promiscuity. If he knows that her soul is less than lily-white, if he knows she is capable of complication and deception and experimentation and lust, then union with her puts him in peril. Women think like children, forgive like mothers, don't plan ahead like kittens. Lennon's first wife, Cynthia, fit the image of the soul-saver angel of olden days. Blonde, young, taking a backseat, maternal, compliant, unambitious, un-idea'ed, warm, pliant. Yes, dear.

Yoko, on the other hand, got into John's finances. She got into his head. She got into his creative decisions, his social beliefs. And he into hers. Yoko was the first and last female allowed into a Beatles session, and even gave vocals on "Bungalo Bill" and ideas on "Revolution 9." All the men but John seethed. Paul McCartney reportedly spat out the vocals "Get Back" straight at Yoko, hate in his eyes. This behavior is ridiculous to me now. Artists collaborate with each other all the time, and all that incredible creative male energy could not be ruined or broken by a few peeps of feminine energy, feminine point of view, feminine sounds. The Beatles had been together a long time; surely their alliance was not so fragile that it would tear apart from a tiny influence that was different. If they were open, they could have taken it in and made themselves a little more complicated, a little more mutable. But if I put myself in the mind-set that went generations back where to let women into business, into your work process, was to dirty the woman and therefore damn your combined souls...

Yoko Ono ruined centuries of social conditioning that had, unknown to him, ossified some channels of thought in John Lennon's head. Yes, Yoko is like LSD. Except an acid trip only lasts maybe twelve hours. Yoko goes on and on.

WHAT IS THE SOUND OF NO HANDS CLAPPING?

My friend David Cotner says, "Silence in music is an affront to the Protestant work ethic. It angers people. Makes them think they're not getting their money's worth."

The Slits, an English band attuned to island people's meshing with nature, sang: "Silence is a rhythm, too!"

Yoko did not strum and sing at us to listen to the sound of silence, which for her was "the sound of fear and darkness"— she gave us silence, directly, and it became ours. She didn't try to create something out of it and put her stamp on it. She tried to let it stay itself, and give it—nothing—to us pure.

Nineteen sixty-nine's *Unfinished Music No. 2: Life with the Lions* bore a cover image of Yoko in a hospital bed, John by her side; they'd just lost their baby. One track was two minutes of silence. John Cage, with whom Yoko worked in the '60s in New York, had written a score called *4'33"*, where all the instruments in the orchestra were instructed to not play. In recordings of the performance, you can hear the audience moving in their seats, coughing. Enactment of his idea forced the audience to reassess what "audience/listener" and "performer" mean. Take charge of your life! "Every seat is the best seat"—in life as in the music hall. As Cage's players didn't play, you were forced to shift your perspective or focus off the stage. It is a very uncomfortable feeling, to not be entertained. Hopefully what follows is a shift in values and beliefs and understanding or empathy... the satori after the uncalm.

Friend David Cotner made the distinction: "Cage's silence was about process, while Yoko and John's was about substance."

Cage was a teacher. Ono was being personal in public. The experience Cage gave his audience was an opportunity to confront one's expectations about roles, about being amused, about passivity or receptivity, about accepting what's on the screen or stage or your to-do list instead of, in place of, living, seeing, hearing. I believe that Ono, on the other hand, was expressing herself, her feeling, her loss. Ono's silence was her dead baby. Not a lesson. Ono transcended teaching us about silence or life or ourselves. Ono simply was doing it.

JUST BEFORE THE SILENCE

"Baby's Heartbeat" was another track on *Unfinished Music No. 2*. It was John and Yoko's baby's dying heartbeats, recorded in the womb. They credited the dead baby for his contribution to the album, along with all the other performing musicians. "John Ono Lennon II." Creepy? Sad? *Crad?*

I guess if you peer closely enough at sorrow, eventually you'll be creepy. And if you get too involved with joy (sounds of lovemaking, for example—what it really sounds like, not the pornographic soap operas of it), there, too, you get creepy. People think there's something wrong with you, to be so involved, so introspective, so filled, with *any* feeling or thought.

JOHN BACKED HER UP WHEN SHE SAID THERE WAS GOOD IN HITLER AND EVERY LIVING THING

They were on their honeymoon, in bed in the hotel, inviting in a largely hostile press, ending war by emanating peace, and disseminating those vibes over the media—media as medium! Ono, already hated for being Japanese, for marrying a Beatle and the band then breaking up, for being hairy, just went for it, expressing her outrageously different viewpoint, seeming to innocently believe that the whole world would suddenly accept her concept of love. No caution at all, no regard of the level of hostility aimed at her and her ways, no sense of self-protection. She said out loud that she believed the holocaust would not have happened if she'd been Hitler's girlfriend. Because, she believed, he needed to be turned on. When you look around and realize everything is perfect, you don't have it in you anymore to want to destroy. Love would have destroyed the destroyer. "The reason why there is war or a dictatorship," she said, "is that people don't give love enough. If everybody loved Hitler, 'love' meaning really communicating and opening his mind and turning him on, then he wouldn't have been there."

The journalists, of course, said, "You're crazy." And John said, "She's not crazy. What did she just say that's crazy?"

Westerners don't look at it—life, how to run life—like that: by what-if alternate realities. The West sees by rearview mirror only. We judge by what people have done, and we don't look to nourish what they could or might do or be. Don't see the good. Plant the fear. Westerners don't really believe people are good. We think we're natural ruffians who have to be frightened of terrible consequences in order to suppress that inherent badness. We murder the murderers. We wage war on warring nations. We send rapists to prison and say I hope you get raped. We react in kind to what has happened already, and in doing so, perpetuate whatever violence we decry.

When you look only at what someone has done and don't see what could be, this allows other people's actions to control our reality. When we vote for the death penalty and our tax dollars pay the executioner, we allow murderers to turn us into murderers. We let the lowest create our personality and our fate. And then we feel we must control other people's reality in order to get control of our own reality back.

My friend's husband, to some uncertain extent, cheated on her. My friend said to her husband, "Delete this person on your Facebook page, or if you don't, we're going to get a divorce, our kids are going to grow up in two crappy apartments instead of one nice house, and everything's going to hell." I think that is a very Western thing to say. My friend is not trying to remind him about loving her. She is trying to scare him into not acting on his love for another, due to the hideous and eternal punishment that will surely result. Not only for him, but for her and the children as well, and the home, and the future. The entire family's fate rested literally in my friend's husband's index finger. Would he hit the delete key or would he hover that finger above it, not hitting? My friend allowed another's tiny action or inaction to determine the reality for four people. This husband, having strayed, destroyed something, but now my friend allowed his destroying to create a destroyer out of her.

I know how scathing/scalding it feels to be cheated on. I'm not suggesting my friend is wrong for feeling screwed over, or that her kids got screwed over. It did happen. But terrible things do. We don't protect ourselves and our families from threats by threatening. That escalates the terror. If attacking attackers worked, we would have solved infidelity, domestic abuse, crime, and war a long time ago.

So why not try another way? Ono is so feminine. Our world is so masculine, it let Hitler's dictatorship rise for years unrecognized, for it was just an exaggerated and perverted form of masculinity run amok. And then it took five years of the Allies pounding on him to finally defeat him...and still they didn't kill him! He killed himself! Yoko wanted to fight Hitler. She thinks she could have done what a million men could not. Stop him. With love. Turn him on.

I've known some murderers. They were very repressed creatively. I think Yoko is right when she says you destroy when that's the only way you can see to create. She said there are two kinds of people. Those "confident because they know they have the ability to create, and [those] who have been demoralized" into believing they're only capable of taking orders, or, if they're lucky or crafty or connected enough, giving orders. If they fall in the latter category, they may feel that the only way to get that knee out of their back is to twist around and strangle the one holding them down. Isn't that what the Nazis thought they were doing? They thought they'd been robbed and demoralized by Jews. They saw robbing and killing Jews as the only way to get back their freedom. Even Nazi art was not allowed to be creative. It had to be "noble" and "realistic" and "beautiful." It was not free. It was not freeing.

Ono wants to wake you up, open you up, release you, inspire you not to admire her artwork or herself, but to admire yourself, your own awakened creative powers. To admire the world as it is, nature, love, man, woman, imperfect all. Perfect all.

People who are oppressed will, given (or taking) the opportunity, oppress others. People who are creative and admiring will make opportunities for others to create; to get ahead by stepping on heads does not occur to them. People are not naturally nasty. Only when they feel cornered.

Yoko said her work was incomplete "to incite people to loosen their oppression" by having to complete it themselves, and finding out they could. Can you picture how hard it is for the artist to leave her work unfinished and put it out there for anyone to put their grubby-fingered, unskilled imagination all over your baby and do God knows what to it, turning it into God knows what? That takes a ton of trust and respect. It's the opposite of a dictator.

Ono is a crazy door opener and time traveler. I imagine her putting her hand on young Hitler's arm and infusing him with that luxurious feeling of not needing to do a thing. Not needing to become something, prove something, control anything. For just one moment. And in that moment, something would have come alive in him. Some awareness or perception and respect for life and people just as they are, with no need to perfect or order, and that is how war is over.

I heard an interview on NPR with a woman who had been approached on a social network by one of the men who had gang-raped her when she was fourteen. Her response was to ask him about what happened, because, like most people severely traumatized in their youth, she doubted her memories, and her part in what happened, and her sanity. He told her it was all true, it all happened. He claimed to have mistakenly thought it was consensual. She did not try to have him prosecuted. Maybe the statute of limitations had run out, or maybe she was just grateful that someone was choosing to tell her the truth and in doing so, help her heal—even if that person was her rapist. What struck me most is that the woman said that what she chose to tell her rapist from long ago, who has three children now, is to teach his daughters to respect themselves enough to stay away from dangerous or exploitative situations, or go to the authorities if it does happen, and to teach his son to respect women enough to stop what he's doing to them at the first sign something is wrong. The way this woman healed the past was to stop looking at it, and instead go into the best possible future.

The usual way in the West is to react to what has happened. Ono is all about what *hasn't* happened. Every piece of her art, every interview, is about *possibility*. Not actuality. Opening doors. Not sticking something on a wall. Knocking a hole in the wall. She knocked a hole in a canvas and told people to look through it. Then she didn't even provide a canvas. Said go get your own, and knock or burn your own hole. Create a hole, become a hole, look through yourself with no barriers (preconceptions are the barriers between you and the living life-ness all around you right now). Look at what isn't yet, and it will be there. Knock down a wall, and stick nothing in its place. Now look and see what was always there to see.

What does this have to do with Hitler, or anyone who may be like him in some small, early way right now? Everything.

When we speak of Hitler, we are not speaking of the living man, or even of a man in any sense of the word. His name has become shorthand for evil, a cartoon of evil, an accrual of all the terrible things he did or ordered done or would have done. There's no complex, conflicted, possibilitied human being left in our discussion of him, but it was that real human being who came to do and, through coercion and charisma and appeal to other real humans' greed, get the cooperation of others to have done all those terrible things. Evil is not Hitler. Evil is evil. Whether it's your country's dictator or your family's head of household, if you're helpless in their clutches and the other people around just watch while you're blamed for the financial situation, exploited, your human rights disregarded and ultimately destroyed, even though it's not on the scale of millions killed, it's still the only scale you know. Your life is your everything.

Right now, leaders all over the world are blaming certain ethnic groups or religious factions or the disabled or the mentally ill and/or addicted or the elderly or the unmarried mothers or the homosexuals or the poor or the abused and acting out for their country's economic, cultural, or criminal problems. And they pretend—if you read around the euphemisms of their speech, like that they want to take away help in order to give the vulnerable and the sick the *opportunity* to help themselves—that to starve and tax and deprive of rights the unfortunates is how the country will get strong again. That's what Hitler told the out-of-work Germans nearly a hundred years ago, and the people agreed. That's what slave owners claimed a hundred years before that, and people purchased that cheaper tobacco and cotton and said okay, yes. And so on, backward and forward in time They say they are helping industry, they are making progress, creating jobs, but really they are destroying.

During the 2012 American presidential primary debates, Republican candidate Rick Santorum was asked why homosexuals shouldn't be allowed the same right to marry as heterosexual couples, and he responded that then we would allow three men to marry, or let men marry dogs. Personally, I question what harm would come from three men or one man and a dog marrying, but that is beside the point I want to make here, which is that Rick Santorum is implying homosexuality, which is apparently not his sexuality, is similar to insanity or bestiality, and should be denied equal rights. Hitler felt that. People who don't agree with Rick Santorum tend to hate him, call him "a fuckwit." Want to destroy him. Which means they're treating Rick Santorum similar to the way in which he wants to treat homosexuals. Ono believes we are not accomplishing anything when we answer oppression with attempts to stomp the oppressors, and in doing so, we believe we free the oppressed. Ono believes the oppressors need to be freed from oppression as much as anyone else.

In the future, our descendants might say how could we not be outraged by and stop the poisoning of our oceans and the genocide of marine life. It's human nature to accept what we're told is normal by the winners of today, and to not see beyond what we are told is right and real. It is dangerous to see and think otherwise. But that is Ono's nature. That is the basis of her career and life: that it would occur to her to picture young Hitler, and to picture giving him love.

How bold, how surprising, how feminine and strong of Yoko Ono to appeal to the good deep inside our world leaders, to offer them love and mail them seeds to plant rather than to launch attacks on their character or to try to steal back what they've stolen. That's a never-ending cycle. Everyone in that cycle feels justified. But it doesn't solve anything or change anything or make anyone happy.

The oppressed hang onto the hierarchy of oppression when they propose treating the violent with violence, treating the robbers by robbing them, treating the cruel with cruelty. There's only one way out of the self-perpetuating structure of hierarchy, no matter where you fall on it. That's to walk out of it. Stop believing it. Picture a big bully like Rick Santorum as tender inside; try to turn him on. So he can discover his own honor and creativity, and not need to find it externally, in coercing others to behave as a mirror to his own (unachieved) ideals of perfection. Then he'll stop coercing. But first you have to stop trying to coerce the coercers. It's a trap, it's a trap! Power over others is a trap, no matter which side of it you're on.

When Yoko made her Hitler comments during her and John's Bed-In in 1969, the journalists she spoke to broke from their professional objectivity and called her crazy right then and there. Forty-five years later, even progressives and liberals attack her idea, and compare it to other far-out stances in lunacy, such as Gandhi saying that if he'd been a Jew in Hitler's Germany, he would have offered himself up for gentiles' bullets to show his moral superiority of gentleness. Well, I have to say, I, too, think *that's* crazy! You don't let murderers turn you into a murderer if that's not what you want to be, but that doesn't mean you offer yourself up as the next victim! Like, you'll teach him a lesson by inviting him to kill you? And that's not at all what Ono was saying. She was going back in time to *before* the mass murders occurred. Do what could have been done back then, attitudes altered, to *prevent* violence and war. Now take that knowledge and apply it today. We have future mass murderers among us right now.

I find it pretty amazing that Ono, identified primarily as a kooky singer, is being grouped with Gandhi—albeit unfavorably, in an effort to discount her thinking—one of the greatest philosophers of passive resistance of all.

We are all foreigners in a new world if we take a step past what we "know." Yoko's art makes us foreigners in our own hometown.

EAST AND WEST

There are many talented people. Phenomenal executioners of art, performance, painting, political rhetoric. There are a million of them. Idea people are rare. And are not loved. We in America do not love ideas that aren't done. We do not love people who can stay in the possibility. They give off foreignness, threat, challenge.

Because Yoko keeps things undone, she keeps things possible. Her ridiculous, unfinished pieces of art or performance are meant to induce satori, to be looked through to what is beautiful, not meant to be beautiful themselves, or to be anything at all. At least, not meant to be made beautiful by her hand. Maybe by yours.

My boyfriend, who is a businessman, has eight big watches and at least that many clocks. Plus calendars and a whiteboard. He puts numbers all over the place, marks everything up into time and date, and all sorts of other information he uses to stitch up the amorphous surge into a sack. Longitude, latitude, what time it is in Paris, the correct name for things, a stopwatch to freeze time. He has name brands, too. They create who he is with the external. He likes the exterior because it can be controlled. The internal just is, and so he keeps it hidden, and can it grow in the dark? My boyfriend is so Western.

The Japanese use space and light and silence as important elements of art and home layout. Western ego needs to fill it all in with our creation, our words, our decisions, our colors and stuff and symbols and trinkets and puffy furniture and squiggles.

My boyfriend hates Yoko Ono.

WHAT A MOTHER SHOULD BE

She had this hands off policy to child rearing and husband loving the same as she did with her art making, where she let everything be exactly as it moved to be. She lets you be the hands and eyes in her art, she lets other people make their own decisions about reality, lets other people make the shape of the relationship or the art piece. And to believe that something must always make its own course means always being ready to walk away, or to let it walk away from you. Yoko allowed her toddler daughter to live much of the time apart from her, sometimes with strangers, in a strange (to Kyoko) country (England). Plenty of parents very dedicated to their careers serially abandon their children and spouses. If they're male. This was a mother in the 1960s.

On parenting Kyoko, she said: "I was sort of an offbeat mother.... I wasn't particularly taking care of her, but she was always with me [when she was little]—onstage or at gallery shows.... I took her onstage as an instrument—an uncontrollable instrument." She has the self-awareness to know that this is not normal, that this is probably not what a child needs, and has the surprising humility to explain that it is because of the dearth of normal, comforting parenting from her mother that Kyoko was closer to her father. I say "surprising" because she doesn't try to justify or excuse her lack of mothering as normal for an artist and therefore part of the patriarchy's plot to keep women down. She threw herself into her work, and biographer after biographer, and even friends, like Gene Mahon, called that "maternal indifference" and "neglect," despite there being a husband—Tony Cox—to look after the house and their child, Kyoko, when Kyoko was small. What did Yoko do wrong? Yet she doesn't ask that question. She doesn't look at it sociologically, justifying her actions in life or inaction in parenting. She looks at it from the child's point of view, and just says it like it is, without regrets, without denial or blame.

She may have realized, with Kyoko, that this nonapproach places too much responsibility on the child to make her own life, create her relationship with her mom. She may have overcorrected with Sean.

Since Yoko refuses to make excuses or demand answers or fairness, I think I will: Would we be having this conversation if the artist was a man, a father? If we required men to relinquish their lust for work and outside life when they had children, our civilization would never proceed in architecture, philosophy, business, travel, art, engineering.

Mothers feel a lot of pressure. Who do you think we take it out on?

Similarly, while Yoko won't complain about her own treatment by society, she does speak up on other mothers' behalf. Yoko will always say what no one else wants to admit. She said, "In general, mothers have a very strong resentment toward their children, even though there's this whole adulation about motherhood.... Women are just too stretched out...."

I'm sure sometimes less control and regimenting doesn't work. Sometimes too much is destructive. Either way you go, the mother questions herself, feels the pressure. It's like there are all these hooks in us of perceptions of us, expectations, each pulling in a different direction. Yoko calmly removed the hooks, and stayed little and solid and self.

What did Yoko do wrong? She broke society's standards. Again. That's what she did wrong. She simply refused those standards of what a mother should and shouldn't be—for better and for worse—and exposed those preconceptions for how binding and strangling they are. She knocked down a wall and showed it was a doorway. Maybe she left that particular door too wide open. She was not a perfect mother. Who is? But while most of us try to cover up our mistakes, Yoko communicates hers, calmly.

I can't walk through the doorway Yoko made for me in the wall, not this time. This book is late and I might get fired. Again. Because my daughter was talking to me all morning about her dream where she was awake with her eyes closed. And because sometimes I'm afraid to leave her or my son with sitters because they may be treated badly. And because I have no trust in people or fate that what happens is right, and I don't know where the path or chain of events leads, and I am not willing to let my children walk down whatever path opens up before them without me knowing what it is and where it's going, but instead I must control what happens to them. And so I have these work ideas trapped inside me, undone, dying. I end up holding tight to both my children and my ideas, and life does not flow through me or them.

But maybe it's not too late. If I wasn't so immersed in Yoko Ono right now, I never would have admitted any of that to even myself, never mind the whole world. Once you say it out loud, though, you realize it's not so bad a thing so as to need to be "admitted." Maybe it's just the way it is. I'm not failing. I *am* mothering, and living, maybe not good *or* bad.

I know a lot about Sylvia Plath's, Anne Sexton's, and Maya Angelou's failings as mothers. Because people—including themselves, the failing mothers—are always talking about them. Yoko does not talk about herself as a failure as a mother. In not judging herself, she bravely stands up and allows me to consider the possibility of not judging myself.

Making the judgment about whether a mother is "good" is like making the judgment about whether a voice is "good." Or whether someone is a good lover. It's just not up for review— your mothering, your voice, your loving. It's not a single performance to be evaluated. It's alive and changing. To give it a verdict is like writing a biography of a child who hasn't finished growing, and deciding their worth by what they've so far accomplished. It's that Western need to put things in their place again—to judge something in the present as if it were a dead thing and its past is all that matters, as if possibility— future ways one could turn, ways perceptions will change— doesn't matter, isn't as much a part of what something is as is what it was.

WHAT A GOOD VOICE HIDES

It's a straitjacket, to think you have to use a "good voice" to express yourself, your emotions, and experiences—whether it's your voice in explaining your beliefs or your voice singing them. And it's a straitjacket to think that if you don't have this era-specific (because it definitely varies from century to century) idea of a good voice, or good message, you can't or shouldn't have or use any voice at all. That's like saying I refuse to write a letter expressing how I feel because I have bad hands! Or I refuse to live and move and fuck because I have a bad body! I don't have anything to do living with except this body; I don't have anything to say anything with except this voice.... Can you imagine stopping yourself from... *anything*...because you have the wrong body type for your era? You better believe in reincarnation if you're going to repress yourself from anything because you don't fit into the currently fashionable, because this is your one shot! Yoko never let her voice being reedy or her message being hated and dismissed stop her.

Those of us with "good" voices and messages are expressing the right mores and emotions and experiences—romance—of our times. Or rather, echo expertly the lonely, crazy groundbreakers that came just before us. Doo-wop for innocence. Pop for nostalgia and future fantasies. Rock for lust and a mob's propensity for violence. Jazz for nervous jiggling of the soul's foot. Blues for sultry, graphic, wet, rubby—or lack thereof, and an equally sultry longing for what's just out of reach.

Vocals for Yoko had always had a more expansive definition than for others. Screaming, whispering, nothing, harsh, weak, fear, love. Sounds without words to cage them. Without melodies to control their direction. Without rhymes to force them. She frees them from being named (which is what words are and do to emotions and perspective). Once something is named, it is known, it is controlled, it can be discarded. Yoko keeps it primordial.

Asked about her vocalizations unherded into words and seeming so sexual, Yoko said: "I do these sexual sounds, but these sexual sounds could also be someone who is being tortured."

Words on sounds are like cloaks, like peasant dresses, like suits. You see the suit on the subway, you no longer need to see the man under the suit. You know him. You know his kind. You know your relation to his kind. Yoko's noises were naked, often not wearing any words at all, never mind a familiar set, or outfit, of words, rhymes. Her emotions could not, therefore, be dismissed as this or that. That made people uncomfortable. They attacked her. They said she was screaming, she was ugly, she was crazy. They did not like to be forced to see someone else as a real person without definition, and so they made up their own definition, threw it on her like a blanket on a fire, tried to put her out.

PROOF

In 1996 came "Rising Mixes," Yoko's collaborations with alternative musicians Cibo Matto, Ween, Tricky, Thurston Moore, Perry Farrell, Beastie Boys, Le Tigre.... DJs, such as the Pet Shop Boys and Danny Tenaglia, started remixing her stuff for dance clubs in 2002. In 2007 *Yes, I'm a Witch* was released: remixes and covers of her back catalog by various artists, including the Flaming Lips, Cat Power, DJ Spooky, Peaches.

That her songs could be—and have been! no matter the era—remade, reinterpreted, reconstructed, proves that she created real songs. They weren't just chaotic stupidity, base, experimental self-indulgence. She made *songs*. Structures. Stories. That can be taken on and retold, refolded in a new way to make a new creation... because there's so much there to begin with.

Accept impermanence with totality and the impermanence reaches permanence. Or, rather, perpetuity.

BUT IS IT GOOD?

A few of her songs are simply beautiful, seemingly by mistake. She tried to hide them, but they snuck out of her. Sometimes her paintings, instructions, or performances can create awe in the person partaking in them. But for the majority of her work, I don't think you're supposed to *like* it, and I don't know if anyone does. John Hopkins, a fellow artist, said her Happenings were boring and that Yoko Ono was "the most boring artist I'd ever met."

Well, in my opinion, to be the MOST *anything* is mission accomplished. The artist is not here to please.

Anyway, the songs aren't *supposed* to be "good." That's not what they're about. You can hear that she could do a good song if she wanted to. "Nobody Sees Me Like You Do" is almost pretty; it's definitely lovely. It's so close to "right." But still something nags....There is a tear somewhere in the premise of the song. Perhaps it's nothing more complicated than her accent or phrasing—the native English-listening ear is made aware of effort? (Our language is so dominant worldwide, many Americans don't see the need to learn another language or even be bothered to work out someone's unique inflections.) I looked up the lyrics, and what they expressed turned out to be exactly what I'd heard in her voice even when I couldn't make out all the words: gratefulness, with a sense of the still-missing. "Even with our dreams and yearnings, feeling of loneliness hangs over like a thirst. No one can see me like you do. No one can see me like you do." She had it all, but all wasn't enough. How lonely. And how delicately she expressed this ephemeral complaint that is no complaint.

Some producer could have smoothed a "good song" out of her if she let him, I'm sure. That wasn't what she wanted. She wanted to find something out—what could happen; what could be. Always. Stretch the boundaries of what is a song. What is this feeling, truly? We know what we think a song is. We know what we think is the nature of just about every feeling there is. We don't.

Even when totally trying to be normal, what she thinks is normal, she can't. "Intellectuals trying to communicate with people usually fail," she realized, rethinking her entire career in the late '70s. She decided music was about "simple, human feelings," which she would now express "in simple language. No bullshit. If I want to communicate with people, I should use their language. Pop songs are that language."

It's interesting that she calls the language of human feelings "their" language. As if she's not one of the humans. She feels everything, but at such a distance from herself, or from us, or just from such an unusual perspective, it's like it's anthropological.

SURPRISE!

You know who her music reminds me of? You're never going to guess this one: Brian Wilson of the Beach Boys. That alienated reaching out, such need, never meetable.

Or Sinead O'Connor. Her voice and words about freedom and safety would not be so beautiful if she were getting enough of either in life or in her head. She would just be living it. Celebrating or honoring a feeling or situation is over quickly. When the prospect of ever reaching it appears hopeless, it is equally quickly dropped and walked away from. Longing for what you've had little tastes of goes long. We honor and obsess and focus our talents on recapturing the, to us, never quite—but almost—capturable.

Yoko also reminds me of the author Denton Welch. He suffered a spinal injury at twenty that would eventually kill him, and spent the years between his accident and his death describing his walking tour at eighteen in such vivid detail. Love and peace seem to be what Ono cannot hang onto, and refers to so lovingly, yearningly. That feeling of connection and having, all her art talks about it, the same way Welch or Proust, confined to his room in ill health, remembering the high society in which he once mingled, keep going over the feeling of walking, visiting.

Mono no aware is the Japanese term for awareness of impermanence, and appreciating beauty the more for being fleeting. Seeing the flower starting to brown at the edges and knowing it's about to drop but it still has its center color and it's still hanging—you love it the most in that moment. Yoko seems to feel this all the time. The feeling of being about to lose, and feeling just how beautiful is this thing about to fall. She said: "You don't want to possess anything that is dear to you because you might lose it." For the artist, to understand is to possess. She constantly tries to get closer to the thing she is pushing away, to get the inevitable over with.

So awkward with the humans, when you're trying to be true. She's the outsider, the freak, the fly. Small and annoying and everywhere and nowhere. Yoko is emotionally alienated, poring over human interaction from a place where she just can't reach or do it.

She alienates others when she's reaching out most desperately because she's showing just how raw like a wound she is. And she half wants to stay there. She is afraid of what will happen to her if she does reach anyone. They might be taken away.

Maybe she's different today. She seems happy.

LIKE WHAT YOUR ELBOW OR KNEE FEELS LIKE WHEN YOU'RE THROWN OFF A MOTORCYCLE AND SLIDE TEN FEET

Just when you're lulled by the almost-normal handful of songs, she'll come out with something like "Why," which sounds like a turkey forced to watch his mate being held down and decapitated. The energy is infuriated, and...just ...*energy.* It's not a call to revolution. It feels like revolution. Happening. Explosions. Now. Inside.

Iggy and the Stooges made that sound, too. The growls, gasps, moans, and screams erupting all out of *Funhouse*—are they desperate or celebratory or everything at once?

It's not *about* revolution, any more than silence is about silence. It's revolution. It's not *about* the pain of senselessness. It *is.*

"When your mother asks you to do something, I don't want to hear any more 'whys,'" the stepfather boomed, looking scary, looming. "We're the adults. You're the child. You don't ask why." You don't ask why, the officer said to the anarchist.

You don't ask why, the boss said to the employee. You don't ask why, the critic said to the experimenter, and then they called them boring. We're the authority. You have no power. And it's true that a policeman does have the authority to enforce the law and you can't go against him. Those QUESTION AUTHORITY bumper stickers kind of forget consequences. But perhaps what has been lost is questioning internal authority, how you think. When you stop asking why inside yourself, what's your use anymore as a living thing just in itself, when you're not fulfilling some task to keep business rolling?

The German band Can mewled and hollered and banged. Early Pink Floyd, too. Why is that considered innovative and cool, but Ono was made fun of for doing the same? I think because all those guys are guys, and she is a mother who lost her child, so mewing and screaming are seen as immature, inappropriate, and maybe even endangering.

MESSING UP THE OLD ROCKERS, SHAKING UP THE OLD ROCK

Yoko often mixes things up and just goes with it, like when she and John released a live show they'd done with the Mothers of Invention and didn't get all the credits or anything "right." Frank Zappa was bitter about it even decades later. There was a last-minute live jam at the Fillmore between the Mothers of Invention, John, and Yoko, in 1971. It seems the band was playing the melody of "King Kong," John was singing (loosely) the lyrics of "Baby Please Don't Go," and Yoko added, as various reviewers described, her signature "pig squeals," "tortured cat noises," and—most simply—"fuck donkey."

I think you have to be musically illiterate to believe that she got in the way of these two rock geniuses with her animal sounds. I thought the whole purpose of rock was to wake the animal within? Her animal was wide awake! Anyway, her contributions certainly shook up an otherwise rather pat and solid jam, this animal spirit crashing the masters' meeting.

A year later, John took the masters to Phil Spector to mix, and the Plastic Ono Band released it on *Some Time in New York* as "Jamrag." Frank Zappa was incensed that they'd "changed the thing around." He wanted it to be called "King Kong" and get writing and publishing credit for the Mothers. But didn't they come together and make something new? John did not credit it as "Baby Please Don't Go." Yoko did not credit it as "My Animal Calls." Phil Spector did not credit it as "My Wall of Unfitting Sounds." Zappa called what they did to the jam "a bunch of show business crap." He feels that he is the artistic free spirit and they're the robbers and changers of his intellectual property. It didn't occur to him that artistic freedom may exist only when no one hangs on too tightly to the past, to a form. Everybody else was trying to create something new out of varied elements. Zappa seemed to believe they were just repeating the same thing they—the Mothers of Invention—had done so many times before.

Yoko Ono on letting people touch her work, her face, her body, complete her work, change her work: "I was a war child. Life was transient, and often with sudden changes. I was always forced to move on. Static life seemed innately false to me."

And when she, this unbeloved, yelping small foreigner, found herself onstage with two giants, icons, rock gods, she was not intimidated by their body of work, their history, their belovedness. This was just another moment, another chance to capture something new before letting it go.

Zappa and Lennon were just jamming when Yoko opened it all up. It was like she was vomiting her vocals. It was shocking. And isn't that the definition of rock, at its most primal? It erupts. It's not neat. Rock does not come from the head. Rock does not make sense. Rock comes from down below.

Ego is the need to be correct in our interpretation of reality at any moment. But reality is fluid. It takes many faces. And so we try to freeze it. Unable to accept the limitations of our mind, we try to place limitations on the reality. Artists, historians. History is not dead! String theory!

LIVE PEACE IN TORONTO, 1969

Another rock genius union she was supposed to have messed up with her annoyingness is that of Eric Clapton and John Lennon. "I was trying to enjoy the song," everyone complained about "Cold Turkey" as performed by Clapton, Lennon, Klaus Voormann, Alan White, and Ono, "but Yoko wouldn't shut up."

This was the first time John Lennon had been onstage without the Beatles. Why did anyone want to hear something that sounded *like* the Beatles but could never be as good? There was all this pressure on Lennon. He was the one who broke up the band. He grew up with those guys, as had probably every single person in that vast audience. In an effort to calm Lennon and Clapton, who had been on a plane, possibly junk-sick, for about twelve hours, producer/manager/songwriter Kim Fowley, seeing how scared the guys were, got everyone in the crowd to hold up their lighter or candles he'd given them when the newly formed band walked onstage, and everyone did. It was the first time. Lennon must have been so grateful to have Yoko there, someone so unique and powerful artistically forming something up there with him that would, no matter what it did turn out as, never be a pathetic imitation of what he had achieved musically before. No matter how good or bad something was with Yoko Ono, it wouldn't be a copy!

"Cold Turkey" is John singing about kicking heroin—the fevers, pain, sweat, cramps, shitting your pants, bargaining with God, begging, being plagued by doubts.... He's singing the words about it; she's singing the sounds of it. She's singing *it*. How much safety of distance should there be for the listener in a song describing an addict's suffering?

CHUCK BERRY WAS SHOCKED

People were incensed that John would "take his wife to work" on *The Mike Douglas Show* when he got the opportunity to play with his idol, Chuck Berry. What? Yoko was a musician and singer, just like everybody else on that stage! She'd been on stages making music and other performance for twenty years. No, for nearly forty years, since she was a small child, classically trained! For most of this gig, she just quietly played bongos and kazoo while John and Chuck Berry hashed out the latter's hits. At one point she lets some squawks out, and I think it's hilarious! The look in Chuck Berry's eyes! He couldn't believe it! But I think he thought it was a little funny, if crazy—her sudden turkey call. I think he may have liked it! He was an innovator and expressive and wild and squawky and not right himself. How could he fail to appreciate all those things in someone else? Her turkey call was the most alive moment, or at least the only surprising one, in what otherwise would have been just a fairly perfect repeat of what had been created long ago, like reading sheet music and hitting it note for note.

BASTARD

The song "What a Bastard the World Is" is on Ono's album *Approximately Infinite Universe*, which came out in 1973. It begins with the lover coming home late, walking quiet and peeking in to see if he's caught, see if he's in trouble. "Slowly the door opens, you stand for a while, see if I'm asleep or just closing my eyes." We've all pretended to be asleep sometimes to avoid being seen in pain. We've all pretended to believe the other person really is sleeping to avoid seeing their pain. There is much pain in love, and much pretending. But she opens her eyes this time—she stops the pretending, she jumps up, throws pillows and a full ashtray, full of her night's waiting, her night's worrying. She explodes: "You jerk, you pig, you bastard, you scum of the earth, you good for nothing...Oh, don't go, don't go! Please! Don't go!" That classically trained vibrato, the complicating accent, she is Yoko Ono singing this song, she is telling this waiting woman's story using the anger and feminism she believes in, and then it all drops, Yoko Ono loses herself, her early opera lessons, her beliefs and intentions, and even her accent. She melts completely into soft and whispering woman-plea universal, without country, without class, without story: "I didn't mean it. I'm just in pain. I'm sorry. I'm sorry."

She can't go on like that. She'd drown. She switches to third person. She steps outside the agony and peers down into herself, her story, as if she, the storyteller, were an alien observer.

Still not enough distance. She now separates from being or telling the story of any one woman at all, or any one man, and flies far up, far away, until her scope is wide enough to see that it is the world who is the bastard.

This is one of the best songs ever written!

John Lennon didn't want her to release it because he didn't want everyone to think it was about him. But as usual, Yoko cared more about the piece, the song, the message, than she did about one person's wishes or feelings. Whether that one person is herself, her beloved, or an enemy. Or a million people's wishes (that she'd shut up)! Or the media's. Or a nation's. She was single-minded in her dedication to tell what is true, or not tell what is not true, no matter how inconvenient or unattractive. No matter how her station in life changed, her perspective did not adjust accordingly. I remember my boss at a fish stand advising me to be Democrat while I was young and barely making money and switch to Republican once I had it and wanted to keep it. Yoko changed. She never switched.

She is the most open and most closed woman there is.

MEN

She is so unique, so creative and not reflective—so not an appendage, and yet, even now, the media and the public identify her with men. Men are one half of the population! How could she have avoided them all? And why should she have to, to be judged on the merits of her ideas? Male artists consort with women. Even an art magazine, *Artnet*, identifies her Bed-Ins for Peace as "with the Beatle" and *Cut Piece* as "provocative Fluxus actions." But Yoko was the one who got "the Beatle" into nonviolent guru-ish activism for peace, and Fluxus wasn't even named, or formed, until 1961, when Yoko had already been planning and doing Happenings for years!

In researching this book, I asked everyone I ran into what they knew of Yoko Ono, and they'd say she was with John Lennon. But *he* was with *her*. She influenced and changed and expanded him much more than he did her. She was doing things like Bed-Ins for a long time before she met John. She got *him* into art, into feminism, into insurrection. In the 1970s, she got them intimate with radicals. Bobby Seale, Abbie Hoffman, Jerry Rubin, Michael X, John Sinclair, Angela Davis. They even held a concert as a fund-raiser to try to get one of them out of prison.

Duchamp and Max Ernst attended her first concert, in 1960. She did not speak to them. She was doing stuff with the members of Fluxus before they were Fluxus. She met John

Lennon in 1966. She'd already married a composer ten years earlier. She'd already been in a mental institution. She'd been around. To agree to the tenets of an organization, no matter how loose, artistic, and humorous, whether in the form of a romantic collaboration or a named collection of the like-minded, would have squeezed too tightly what she wanted to express and how. Most of the time she didn't even know what she wanted to happen before it happened, as she'd leave so much of art and life and love undone for someone else to finish, to do, to have room in which to move and be and move again.

JOHN RIPPED *HER* OFF!

Shortly after they got together, John suddenly had an art opening, which *she'd* been doing already for years, and he copied her "Yes" concept! He later admitted that he'd used some of her ideas in his music without crediting her.

Yes, imitation is the sincerest form of flattery, and anyway, everybody rips off everybody. There are only so many ideas. One must cannibalize, as an artist, or idea-starve. And Yoko didn't mind.

But culture should ask itself why them getting together is known as her destroying his band, instead of getting him into more experimental, raw art and music. And yet no one says he destroyed her art, even though she got off course from her instructional and experimental art and more into comprehensible music. And what if her influence did hasten the demise of a band that had been going on a really long time and instead catalyzed the creation of something new and challenging and intriguing—John's solo musical and artistic career, and a foray into activism, and an experiment of what happens when man and woman, East and West, truly mix, consume and give freely, and become one new, fascinating hybrid?

A FILM CALLED
RAPE

The film *Rape* by Yoko and John—it was Yoko's idea—features a girl they picked out at Hyde Park. A cameraman follows her, filming her increasing disturbance mercilessly. The victim was Hungarian and spoke no English. Her torment lasted seventy-seven minutes. It was Yoko's sixth film and came out in 1969.

Now, it would be illegal to make that film. Unless you're Homeland Security post-9/11. Then you can pick a girl out at random and with no subpoena, no just cause, you can track her movements from various traffic and store cameras, her cell phone, her GPS, and you have carte blanche to enter her home, office, computer, and never even tell her you did it.

That would be a good film to make today, and call it *Rape*.

Yoko Ono's films may have been about something esoteric, but they told that ethereal story through a few body parts, close up, slowed down.

Film One, 1965, was a hand striking a match in slow motion. It took five minutes.

Bottoms was...bottoms. I guess we're all the same underneath? And I do mean *underneath*.

The 1966 version of *Bottoms* lasts five minutes. The 1967 version is one hour and twenty minutes long. She met Lennon in 1966, and he immediately began funding her ideas, enthusiastically. There you go, that's what money can buy. One hour, fifteen minutes more bottoms!

Freedom, 1968, is a close-up of a bra with its middle being tugged, about to be ripped open by the wearer, in slow motion, and ends just before it tears.

Up Your Legs Forever, 1968, moves the camera from various men and women's legs from the feet till a microchip away from the genitals. You hear a man on the phone trying to convince more people to come in. A woman argues about whether she'll wear underwear or not. Two people drop "theater of cruelty" references. While watching untorso-ed legs, you hear disembodied voices cooperating or conflicting on this absurd idea—to film legs—with no one dictating how it goes, what is good. Voices separated from faces, legs separated from top halves, discussion separated from persuasion or rule—it's all disembodied. This movie has no plot, no dialogue to read, no eyes to emote. No direction. It puts participants and viewers alike in the uncomfortable position of having no setting, no backdrop, no context. How to distinguish one thing or one position from another, or where on the ladder?

Oh! Hey! What's that? I was watching while writing, and suddenly an artificial leg appeared. I never really looked at one before. And then a different woman appears to have no toes. I wonder what happened. Frostbite? The mob? My mind wanders. No one is pointing which direction it should take. I find the endless legs to have a similar effect as did the endless snow in *A Walk to Taj Mahal*. Neither is a "real" film the way watchers understand. Each is an experience. Or, rather, a nonexperience. Like being dead, maybe. No plot, no logical sound. Nothing to look at, nothing to hear, nothing to think. Only what is already inside you. Maybe some thought you tucked away and forgot about will unfold itself and walk out of its dusty corner that it thought was its grave. But everything is reversed now. Maybe this *is* what it's like to be dead: all the things come to life that had no purpose, no profit, in life.

EQUAL OPPORTUNITY

They made films (plural!) of John Lennon's penis.
Actually, no. I thought there were two because one was of his penis achieving erection, in 1969, which they called *Self Portrait*, and another (in 1971) was called *Erection*, but it was actually a building achieving erection. It took forty-two minutes to show the penis going up and only twenty minutes for the building to go up. Because they did super slow motion on the former and time lapse on the second. *Erection* is haunting. The soundtrack was Yoko making pain noises, moans. It feels like there are souls trapped within the walls. They actually showed these films. An audience at the Institute of Contemporary Arts in London sat there with a Beatle's penis all big across the huge screen, for all that time, in increments getting bigger and bigger and bigger.

In 1968, Yoko filmed *Smile*, which was the corners of John Lennon's mouth rising. The film was so slowed down it took almost an hour. Yoko wanted to make *Smile* five hours long, but ultimately decided that was impractical. When it screened at the 1968 Chicago Film Festival, half the audience made it through at least the first thirty minutes, and got to see his eyebrows wiggling, too. The ones who walked out—weren't they curious how it would end?

There's one more film of something going up: *Apotheosis*, 1970. Hot-air balloon.

Things rising.

There's room in Yoko's world for male energy.

Or just plain energy. As she said to *Esquire*, there is no good and bad power, there is only power. Maybe there's no male and female energy. There's only energy and lethargy, and each can eat the other. You can stay in the Ouroboros (that snake-swallowing-its-own-tail cycle) or you can get up and get out. Nineteen seventy was also the year of *Fly*. The camera follows a fly walking over a naked woman. Then follows the fly as it flies out the window.

OUT

My life is hellish right now, I thought. *I just got slammed into in traffic and my head aches and my rear suspension fell off, along with my exhaust and taillight, and I have to take a taxi to pick up my daughter and it's almost Christmas so everyone is taking taxis and there is none for over an hour and I need one in half an hour. My boyfriend stayed out all night last night.* In my head these things were like an avalanche. So instead of doing the things I was supposed to be doing just now, I was stuck here waiting, and I flipped through various Yoko Ono films and ideas and soundtracks on my computer, and it made me feel more and more like I was rising, like a skyscraper or John Lennon's penis or the hot-air balloon, out of my problems and looking down wondering why ten-minutes-ago me, or anyone, would feel such fuss. Come out. The air is fine.

Yoko's always been a way out for me, from the moment I encountered her work, in 1985 as a sixteen-year-old. My father was in and out of prison and my mother was on welfare and a lot of pills. I was in a small town exploring the library, looking for escape routes, looking for other worlds that must have existed only no one had told me about them yet. Maybe subterranean tunnels inhabited by pre-apocalypse dwellers. Underground sex trade. A Mars colony. A secret Masonic sisterhood, hidden in plain sight. I was determined to find a place or a way to live, and go there, and not be like, or live like, or believe like, anyone around me. I found expressionism, Ziggy Stardust, Walt Whitman, Frank Lloyd Wright, punk. I took a bus to a town that had a used record store and I found Yoko Ono's *Season of Glass* for 25 cents. It came out in 1981, and this was four years later, but the record appeared unplayed. This was the pre-digital age, when how loved an object was showed in how worn down it was. And just how alienating this album was shined in its pristine condition. I took it to my friend's house and listened to it—seemingly like the previous owner—one time only. It was horrible. And memorable. I didn't know why this woman was doing things the way she did, so unpleasantly.

On the cover were smashed spectacles with blood on them that my friend told me were John Lennon's, who had been married to Yoko Ono (the Beatles meant nothing to me, as they belonged to my parents, and I wanted nothing that was theirs). And a half-filled water glass.

Now I think the significance of that half-drunk glass of water was a demonstration of impermanence. He was there, gulping at it, and then he was gone, and the second half of the water was still there, waiting for him, waiting and waiting. Undrunk forever. Frozen unfinished. I never saw water look sad before. But at that time of my life, I was not interested in connections that got broken; I was not interested in love. I wanted out. I wanted everything that existed broken, to make way for the new. Why was this woman making these things?

The song "No No No" reminded me of *Peter and the Wolf*, a play I'd seen as a child. She was a miserable crone saying let me take my wig off, don't touch me, and something about doing it. Then the music turned New Wave, with a *boi-i-ing* bouncy sound, and her voice transformed to operatic, beautiful—for a single line: "You promised me." Over and over she cries that line out in a mighty voice over swelling keyboards (yes, *two* keyboardists employed on this song, as well as a vibraphonist). Who promised? Promised what? Why did she sound so disappointed? Everybody knows no one keeps promises. And yet, she sounded so determined.... I thought about what promises might be like out there in the unknown world.

Now I understand the song "No No No" was about what it felt like trying to have sex for the first time after watching her husband get killed. But married love and making love and being a widow were all so far out of my scope of experience or interest at sixteen, I didn't comprehend anything except the angry pain, which I comprehended completely, and it made me very uncomfortable, because I didn't want to understand that.

At least I thought I understood now that the song is about widow sex. I read someone else's interpretation that it's about being so disconnected from your own physical existence, you think your hair is a wig.

I looked up the lyrics just now; there is no wig. She's saying "ring." She's taking off her wedding ring, not a wig. I love mondegreens.

She has meant so many different things to me as I've grown and changed, but really, every reincarnation she takes in my heart is always the same thing: a doorway made out of what I thought was a wall. It's just the shape of the trap she helps me out of that changes through the years.

LONELY

Union felt strange to Yoko. When she met John, she had just about gotten down how to take loss as gain, traps as new doors opening, and loneliness as congress with the universe. Now here was love and respect and support just for her inside this *one* man's body, inside this *one* life. How precarious that must have turned everything, just when she was starting to feel balanced.

She once described art as communication where desperation intersects with imagination. "Even the best artist, if they don't have the necessity, they will be dried up and they won't have any imagination." She said she has to be lonely to be creative—feeling separate even from her child. The primary reason she gave for sending her husband away to Los Angeles for a year and a half was that upon being with somebody twenty-four hours a day, plus always in the public eye, "I lost the freedom." Yoko said, "I felt castrated. My artwork suffered" from the constant exposure—to the public and to each other. She sent her love away. And she recorded the slight (waif-y, bony-feeling) album *Feeling the Space*, which had no Lennon on it at all except for one track, and included such dark, black-souled songs as "Yellow Girl" and "Coffin Car" and the uncharacteristically sarcastic "Men Men Men."

When relationship problems arise, Yoko says, she doesn't struggle and work on it. She "splits." She focuses on something else. In Lennon's absence, she studied Buddhism, New Age philosophy, business and finance, toured Japan with her band.

But in his absence, the art didn't really come back. And when John came back, still the art did not. Yoko had lost the one thing that had always been hers. And so she did what any idea person would do. She changed the composition of what is art again. Instead of encouraging others to complete art in their minds that Yoko started in hers, she now kept the circle inside her own life, and made art out of non-art, and didn't even communicate at all.

She made art out of studying religions and business. Art as life.

John and Yoko's child, Sean, was born in 1975. There was a big energy crisis; punk broke. John and Yoko were not relevant anymore, nor were they breaking new territory in music. They'd run out of imagination. To their credit, they didn't flog a dead horse or cash in on the past. Both of them went far outside their identities in their fields, in their lives. John re-created himself as a househusband and Yoko became a maker of money—life as art. Not just making money with music contracts, but she invested in farms and Egyptian artifacts.

MONEY

"The first time I visited America was when I was two and a half years old," Yoko said. "That was also the first time I met my father [...], a banker who got to be very important. I used to have to make an appointment to see him."

She was rather unfathered, to put it lightly. Though that's just me putting it any way. She doesn't judge or look for redress. Instead of seeking her father's love or approval directly (which seemed a doomed proposition), Yoko made herself like her father in the late '70s, and then loved herself through herself as him. (This hypothesis is strictly mine. Yoko doesn't talk like this—Western therapy-speak. I think it is too blame-y for her, and too historical and dwelling.) She definitely did not go the neglected-daughter-with-daddy-issues third-party route of finding an older, controlling man. She seemed to try instead, off and on throughout her life, to *be* him as a way to get close to him, without requiring the actual him or even a stand-in.

With her superstar husband staying home to watch the baby and bake bread, Yoko became the banker of one fortune. She quadrupled it.

John Lennon, 1980: "When I was cleaning the cat shit and feeding Sean, she was sitting in rooms full of smoke with men in three-piece suits that they couldn't button."

Yoko approached money management the same way she'd approached everything in her career: conceptually. "I was doing it just as a chess game," she said. "Not on a Monopoly level—that's a bit more realistic. Chess is more conceptual." Doing things conceptually means like 4-D. The beyond-possible dimension.

But, being Yoko, she would find her father not so much through acquiring his characteristics, but by mirroring his losses. Including letting slip away her own daughter, Kyoko, much as he had let slip Yoko. Her father lost his freedom when he was locked up as a POW. Yoko lost her freedom when she was locked up in a mental institution, and later, Yoko's outspokenness cost her years of green-card denial. Yoko's father lost his country repeatedly by moving for years at a time until no one place was home. So did Yoko. Her father lost his love of music—he was a pianist—by becoming a banker and supporting the family. Up until Sean's birth, Yoko sacrificed everything, willingly gave up whatever was not already taken by force, by fate, and allowed all the loss to just flow... by hanging onto the one thing she believed was all hers, was inside her, was her: her career in art. And then she lost that, when she lost her faith in it, or it lost its faith in her as its conduit.

I think of that weird, brief '80s/'90s New Age movement that said moneymaking is art. Chris Kraus wrote about that, and other Semiotext(e) authors. Even in giving up art for art's sake (temporarily) and getting all moneyed, Yoko pioneered. Avant the avant-garde!

A BORN WIDOW

I was brought up Protestant. There was nothing protesting about it. I was told the answers and then I had to find a way to make the reality fit into what I had been told already that it was. I had to adjust my perspective until I got it "right."

"Why did that father give his daughter to the mob to rape and he gets called a good Christian who loves the Lord?" I asked in Sunday school. ("Behold, I have two virgin daughters. Let me bring them out to you, and you can do with them as you wish. But please, leave these men alone, for they are my guests and are under my protection." Genesis 19:8) I was answered: "Who are you to question the Lord?" So I understood it was right because God said it was right. My thoughts were not wanted. There's a hierarchy, and those closer to the top are allowed to do what they want to those below them, as long as they accept their position below whoever is above them. Adults rule children. Teachers rule children. Principals rule teachers. Police rule principals. The Supreme Court rules police. God rules everybody. And God ruled his child, Jesus, and all children. And police rule children. And so on. That's a lot of weight on an aware child, to be at the very bottom of the enormous pyramid of Everything.

Then I read about Zen masters hitting people with sticks or snowballs—not to punish wrongdoing, but to surprise, to open, to joggle the student out of a pattern of thought into a new thought that led the master knew not where…perhaps to where their authority was superseded, and they would have lost the ability to guide their student. I found that to be incredibly generous and trusting of those masters, to not try to hold onto their mastery, to not fear their students diverging from their path. Then I started taking these Jewish mysticism classes, and the rabbi said don't look for the right answer; live in the question. The question—chaos, uncertainty, change—is where the life is. All the rest is history, and domination.

Before Yoko, tumult in my personal life never interfered with my journalism. I could rid my mind of worry and distraction and get lost in my subject. "I" got lost. Trying to convey Yoko's ideas, I keep coming back to my own situation, questioning it through her questions, fiddling with it, as there must be some other way to arrange it to allow me to escape a difficulty by just understanding that it's not a difficulty. I'm having a hard time writing about Yoko's art exactly because Yoko's art is all about directing me (or you) to look at how I'm (or you're) looking at things. She's always changed my life for the open. I say "the open" instead of "the better" because sometimes it's harder to be freer.

In an interview Yoko and John did, they refused to answer questions, but instead asked questions of the audience. Nervous laughter resulted, and some buffoonery, and perhaps some enlightenment, too. Don't follow leaders. Question authority. Kill your idols. The answer lies within. It was there all along. Open your third eye.

Yoko has always been so trusting, like a Zen monk, so open like a question. She trusts that she can say and do anything with love and she will be understood when the time is right. She doesn't need to punish, which means clamping down on the past, and she doesn't need to guard herself, which means distrusting the future, distrusting the universe to turn out just right, exactly as it turns out. She told John, "We can walk anywhere. We can go out to dinner." She did not want to punish or protect herself and John from the public, the press, or evil. Because evil is only made stronger by recognizing and fearing it. Reacting to it means living your life by its rules, which proves to it that its existence is valid, is real. Evil loses its shape when you simply smile at it welcomingly; it melts back into its original goodness when met with love.

And on December 8, 1980, the couple went out to dinner.

Coming home, John Lennon was shot in the back four times.

Yoko was mere feet away. She screamed. She begged. She said, "Tell me it's not true. Please tell me it's not true." Because she is a human being, she is not just her beliefs of nonattachment. She was attached. But more strongly than other people, Yoko Ono *is* her beliefs. Most strongly, she is the belief that loss is life, too. In the years following John's death, she had before her the task of melding her overwhelming feelings of wanting to fight this loss, to decry it, to destroy it, with her philosophy of *not* warring with loss. Mourning is about living in the past. Yoko is all about no past, no dwelling, no self-pity, so she had to find her own way to be a widow, just as she'd made her own way to mother, to stepmother, to wive, to make art, and to live.

There is no hindsight with which to see, when you're truly alive. There's only what's before you in this moment. Yoko was right; they *could* walk anywhere. They *could* go out to dinner. As it turns out, they met death that evening. But they met it walking. They could have avoided death, perhaps, if they'd been running and hiding from it, but they couldn't have avoided it forever, and all that life before the death would have been spent on death, looking for it coming, and *not* seeing what *was* there.

It had always been this way. Stubborn, parented orphan, powerful and lone, childless mother, canvasless artist, humanless lover. Yoko and her loss, getting along with it like it's a friendly traveler. It comes and goes, like the tide, and when the water leaves her, the shore appears, and when the shore leaves her, the water has returned.

It was as if Yoko had been raised and prepped all along the way to be a widow, like some children are destined to be royalty, some born and raised to where they can't be anything but serial killers. To lose the one person who ever understood her seems too much to ask of anyone, but then again, many fates seem too much to bear when examined closely. Yoko bore hers well.

Years earlier, she'd accepted the absence of her child. She said, "Losing my daughter was a very serious pain. There was always some empty space in my heart. When Sean was born, I thought I was given this very beautiful son, so I should just let it go. And I did." Lennon's death was the beginning of Kyoko coming back to her mother. She sent Yoko a telegram of condolence. The shore left Yoko, the water returned.

GIRLFRIEND

Because Yoko's philosophy of "we are all connected, and loss is flow" is her real life and not just words, she lived it. Only four months after Lennon was murdered, Yoko was shacking up with Sam Havadtoy, an interior designer/antiques dealer. That relationship lasted from 1981 to 2001. The loss of her husband, lover, creative partner, co-parent, best friend did not take up space like a wall in her heart nor between her legs to disallow quick entrance of the new.

I don't use that gauche phrasing to imply she's a slut. I don't even believe in the existence of sluts, any more than I believe in fairies. That would assume a woman should be dainty and modest. Yoko was neither; nor was she asexual; nor did she do widowhood with the Joneses' propriety any more than she did *anything* the way anyone else believes she's *supposed* to. I think there's some unspoken rule you wait twelve months after a murder to start doing it again, right? What kind of rule is that? Whom does it benefit? Anyway... statistically, the happier you were in your marriage, the sooner you form a new relationship when your spouse dies. So of course she found someone quickly. But regardless of all that—which is none of our business!—the point is that Yoko does not believe in arbitrary walls, or gates, or time frames for locking and unlocking, or any rules at all. Yoko's no hypocrite. Her beliefs do not float out there, having nothing to do with one's body parts, decisions, or the lives and deaths of strangers and lovers alike. Yoko's beliefs are in her body, and her body is in her beliefs.

Yet... there are consequences for total freedom, wall-lessness. Just as that loss was never a wall that went up, it was also a wall that could never come down. There is a reason the rest of the world lives by rules. We are lost without them. God help me, I'm going to quote Scott Disick (Kourtney Kardashian's baby daddy): "At the end of the day, I have to admit I'm on some kind of leash. And the truth is...I love it. If I wasn't on that leash, I don't know where I'd be." Freedom means no signposts. The reason given for the end of Yoko and boyfriend Sam twenty years later was that she was still with Lennon. When you accept losing as the main force in your life, it doesn't arrest the flow. There is no marker of "Here is the loss. Here the loss occurred." But then, too, there is no marker of "Here the loss stopped. Here the loss was over." If you just go with it—just go with what you find or finds you, just go with losing it, too—you kind of can't ever walk away from getting walked away from. You're kind of stuck by the very ideation of being freed. If you truly accept loss as a part of life, even thinking of it as gaining living, you can't ever really lose...but you also can't lose losing.

PEOPLE AS ART

I must admit I was horrified to hear Julian Lennon's assertion that he was made to pay his father's widow for postcards he'd sent his father. Or that she would sell casts of her husband's bloody death shirt for $25,000 or replicas of his shattered spectacles for $18,000, yet refuse to give Julian any of his father's clothes or guitars. Or any of the $43,000 for the pair of blood items. Wasn't that his father's murder just as it was her husband's murder? Why should she alone profit? Or does she consider that when she used them for art, they were no longer what they were, they were now materials, just like paint or clay or a digital recording? Just as she'd used her life—especially the pain and abandonment parts, but the joy and sensuality as well—as tools, and in doing so, as every artist feels they do, transformed them out of being just pain and into communion. Isn't this the same woman who turned her dying baby's heartbeat and stopped heart into not one but two songs?

She presents ideas of her life so intimately, as microcosms of issues she wants to advocate for or expose. It's like being privy to her loneliness. She is alone, but we are with her aloneness. Neither cancels the other out.

When she uses her murdered husband's bloody shirt in an art piece, I feel like she's talking about grief. Not her grief. That is incidental in her mission. It's world grief she communicates.

She uses the particular, the personal, as a tool or a mirror to the world. She realizes the world is every one of us grieving, fully. She holds up a mirror; we look into our own hearts, not into hers. She tries to reach across the loneliness, but she is slipping away. We are getting closer to secret life, her secret heart. Looks like it, but is not. She is impossible to hold. She is sliding up to you; she is slipping away.

The snippets taken from the intimate life are all tools, and are no more restricted to expressing one life than a guitar in the hands of a bluesman is restricted to expressing the particular events of the player's life.

She uses ghosts like utensils.

MONSTER

Maybe she has to be a monster, really, because no one who already feels connected to people needs to keep trying to build bridges to the humans (bridges made out of art) for sixty, seventy years. Maybe what is ridiculous (and possibly unfeminist) of me is to be surprised. Anyone compelled—really compelled—to do art does so out of an intense sense of isolation. Maybe all artists feel like monsters. And when we feel like one, sometimes we are one.

"No one has ever written, painted, sculpted, modeled, built, or invented except literally to get out of hell." Antonin Artaud.

And who is in hell? Monsters.

Who are monsters? Anyone the herd perceives as not one of them, not one of us, and they are exiled.

WHAT A STEPMOTHER SHOULD BE

But still... I am caught short. To profit off a man's murder and withhold even the neglected child's correspondence, never mind money... I don't understand. How could this kindly, thoughtful fighter for justice (or lier-down for peace) be such a monster? Even if I buy the whole art-as-life, art-in-a-way-more-than-life thing. Art taking the place of life when art becomes life and nullifies art—because then it's all life, it's pure communication. (I do buy that.) Even then... when the deceased's children are forced to picture strangers out there caressing pieces of their father's murder scene, or spotlighting them on a shelf for party guests to see... photos of his father's shattered glasses on album covers in any music store he might walk in, a bloody death shirt cast in some rich people's alcove that he might happen upon, should he attend their party... I think that's offensive. And it's really *hard* to offend me.

Is that what art is—to make even the farthest-out of questioners realize there are some things they're not brave enough to question?

As John's widow, she chose to use his tremendous wealth to buy billboard space and full pages in newspapers and magazines to advertise peace, to be in the spending league of war advertisers. She chose not to give it to Julian Lennon. Why is everyone so angry that she chose the world over the usual death-nepotism? Why is no one asking why John himself didn't leave money specifically to Julian?

STILL MAKING PEOPLE MAD AFTER ALL THESE YEARS

Yoko has not mellowed with the decades. In 2004, she bombed England with little pictures of boobs and vaginas, an homage to Mummy, and then was "shocked" when the BBC and the *Times* said it was offensive and the breasts were removed. What a batty old lady!

Either that, or this is an insane world we live in, and she's simply refusing to give in to the pressure to pretend, along with everyone else, that it's okay to glorify violence as patriotic and exciting, and that nakedness is a dirty thing, a menace.

"I thought I was covering Liverpool with beautiful elements of my mother, or motherhood," she said in an interview in *Contemporary* magazine three years later. "I thought they would love it, the experience of it. You were all born from a woman's body, but you don't want to think about it...."

Maybe it's not women as mothers, as breast-feeders and cuddlers, we as a society are so uncomfortable thinking about. Maybe it's ourselves as small, helpless, needy, cuddled, fed. We're more comfortable with the power position rather than the nurtured.

Why aren't we, and the BBC and the *Times*, finding all these images on our screens and bus stops, taken from movie stills and to promote the news of war and rape and intimidation and degradation offensive and demanding their removal?

Personally, I wouldn't want any of it—the good, the bad, and the ugly—removed. I want everyone's point of view to look at, especially those of people I disagree with, as I have more to learn from them than from those who echo the sentiments I already have. But just stop and think for a second how crazy it is that Yoko's images of motherhood can be removed, and we're killing people on video games and watching them be killed in movies and seeing horror movie ads everywhere, or sex worker newspapers everywhere with just the nipples and the slit covered with black lines, just the parts that give milk and give life. All the rest is okay to be seen.

Yoko refuses to acknowledge that we're not all seeing the breast and vagina as the baby does, as generous and clean and bountiful. But I think she had to be making it up, that she didn't know what would happen with this force-feeding of the female energy on a long-patriarchal society. She disseminated the opposing point of view like planes dropped leaflets of propaganda on the villages with which they were at war! She's trying to change the way things are. She's lucky she didn't get burned at the stake.

The guys won. The nipples were removed. And where babies went with them on the original art, the babies were now opening their mouths to nothing.

I read in one review that the fluttering breasts and vaginas were supposed to be those of John Lennon's dead "mummy"—in her honor on her birthday.

Yoko's years with John were the closest she had to "normal" human connection satisfaction in real time, the closest she got to down to earth, to making concrete, popular songs, the closest she said she ever felt to being understood and supported. After his death, the void reopened. The voices with no voice (loneliness—her own and unnamed others') called again to her, she could hear them in some way other than hearing, and she tried to send messages back to them all, in some way other than the usual methods of communication. She reached out in her old, super-reaching, sometimes overreaching ways, and communicated directly with ghosts, with strangers, with the yet unborn (the future), with loneliness itself.

Everything she did before and after John Lennon was more esoteric, unphysical, weird. Which may be exactly what this world needs. I mean, we certainly have given the legislative, prosaic, and customary routes a good long thousands-year try.

What is the *use* of whispering or primal screams, of shadows or a beam of light, what is the benefit, compared to feeding the poor, banning weapons, exposing the evils of factory farming and genetically modified food organizations? Well... how successful has been our war on drugs, our war on famine, our war on bullying at school, our war on racism, sexism, hate crimes, our war on genocide—all these things we want to abolish? How come they're all still everywhere?

Maybe warring on war doesn't work. Maybe war is just another industry. Maybe the usual protests and specialized art movements are part of the industry, keeping things going as is and has been. Fighting against something, despairing over it, banning it, decrying it, actually kind of feeds it, gives it attention, keeps it going. Maybe it can only be stopped by a beam of light, a rain of mother boobs and vaginas, a film of legs... a fly crawling across a naked lady. Close-up on the fly.

REMEMBER

As I type this, Yoko Ono is seventy-nine years old, in India setting up her new installation, "Remember Us," which consists of casts of beheaded or dismembered women's torsos. News is available everywhere that in some parts of India, as in some parts of the whole world, women are still mutilated, beheaded, or set on fire for committing various crimes like having an affair, getting an education, getting raped, or simply no longer appealing to their husbands. We know this, but it doesn't feel real to us, or it does feel real but it is overwhelming and so we shove it away. We turn away. We think those people, the victims and the people who would—who could—do this to them, are really different, and it's beyond our capacity, outside our duty, to comprehend or to intervene. So we let it happen. Yoko Ono doesn't turn away. She sees neither victim nor victimizer as Other. These women are just like us, except something happened to their bodies, bodies just like ours: They got hacked up. Those could have been our sweet, breathing, caring bodies. She makes casts three-dimensional so that you can touch them, and she's put containers of ash out with invitations to visitors to rub it on themselves. Perhaps ash to put on your forehead between your eyes; perhaps ash like cremated bodies of loved ones.

As with most of her installations through the decades, Yoko sees the violence, the unfairness, the terror, and absorbs it all;

she embraces the reality of it with this sort of cold warmth, and creates art out of it so that we, too, may see tragedy with love, and stand still and acknowledge it, and not turn away in defeat or else retaliate in kind, perpetuating the violence.

Yoko stands outside of time. Her most alive relationship for the last thirty years has been with a dead man. Now that she is an old lady, much of her work reaches out to, or honors obsessively, "mummy"—who wasn't even available when Yoko was a little girl and needed her. It is so haunting to watch footage of her perform *Don't Worry Kyoko (Mummy's Only Looking for Her Hand in the Snow)* to a camera when her living, breathing daughter was kidnapped, hidden, muffled, out of reach. She has a song about loneliness being the only unbearable thing. But she never complains directly about the loneliness as the fault of those who have left her. It's never a curse. She just makes her plaintive howl from the depths of left-ness to art, as art. And she howls for all those who have been left behind, or crushed beneath the wheel.

The echo of that howl, that entreaty to be known, is still heard decades later, remastered, remixed, re-sung, reworked, *and* in its original form, still fresh, still real. Her musical work was vilified or ignored, damned to obscurity at the time she was most prolific, but the remnants of it—the smoke of her fire—blow on and on, long after her more popular and palatable contemporaries slipped into obscurity.

Slightly longer, but similar in essence to the old, small "Yes!" on the ceiling from the 1966 Indica Gallery installation, one wall of the Remember Us installation is covered with "I am uncursed" written in different languages. Most of Ono's fifty-plus years of work centers on making violence toward women or toward anyone palpable, and offering the salve of love, of positive thinking, of saying make it better in your mind and the better will reverberate out. I was thinking that Yoko Ono has so uncursed herself. As an artist, as a Japanese woman, as a wife and mother, she's gotten so much curse from practically the whole world, and she's shaken it all off. She's done for herself the same thing she tries to do for every person on earth: She recognizes the violence (even just of prejudice) aimed at her, she tries to see it for what it really is, and then she tries to absorb the power or energy of the hate and deflect the ugly bent of it, transform it with love and freedom. She is uncursed, she is unleashed. She is not knee-jerk reactive, nor does she retreat. She absorbs, but is not absorbed. Not everyone can live like that—free. Accepting contradiction. Living in the question. I can't think of anyone.

Look at the people you *really* know, who tell you the truth. Are they happy in their marriages, their careers, their neighborhood, with their government? They stay, they believe it when they're told it's supposed to be this way, they don't pursue what they really want—maybe because they're afraid that what they don't know may be worse than what they do. Even when it comes to defending our own or other minority cultures or sexual orientation. We might post a link on Facebook decrying bullying, but if our manager makes a slimy insinuation about a woman and we're up for a performance review, are we really about to do something about it? Freedom for ourselves and others is what we say we want, but it's not how we live. We compromise. You have to compromise a lot to be with someone, or to steer clear of the law, or to not get hated. People complain, but ultimately we believe we have to just accept how it is. Yoko doesn't. She is very idealistic and very brave, through and through—and willing to accept the consequences for her bravery.

Because as much as we are taught, in school, in the family, in the military, that bravery is to be admired, mostly it is hated and feared. It is obedience that is rewarded, because obedience keeps things going as they have been, and that is reassuring to everyone. Bravery is funny looking, suspect, alarming: It shakes everything up and creates doubt. Creates possibility. Obedience is the answer; bravery sows questions. Questions are the opposite of reassuring. They are stimulating to an uncomfortable degree. Questions are where Yoko Ono lives. And she mailed you an invitation to come over. She mailed it on a ray of light, on a whisper, or tucked inside a wish.

LIFE IS BEAUTIFUL

Doing nothing is doing something.
It is often the hardest thing to do.

Unpainted paintings. Unharmonized songs. Superstar crooner remaining quietly at home baking bread while crazy wailer goes out and makes money, makes "music."

Yoko's art is to get all those things out of the way what we unquestionably accept as valuable and dominant so we can see or hear what's already there, but not as ostentatiously deserving to be. Un-alchemy. Making nothing from something. Clear the big trees that you know to make room for the seedlings that you don't.

I still don't know what Yoko Ono is. I know, after listening to and thinking about her for a long time now, a few things I'm not, and life isn't. From what she didn't do and won't be. This is freedom.

I JUST DON'T KNOW WHAT TO SAY ABOUT THIS

In 1994, she produced a musical: *New York Rock*—Broadway renditions of her songs.

WISHING'S FOR SUCKERS

Despite everything I've written about accepting flow, and Yoko's positivity, and...I am in a quandary over what to think about Yoko's wish trees. They're these trees where you write down your wish and tie it to a branch. Just...this...tree...full of wishes. I am so embarrassed by the naïveté. The idea that wishes matter for adults. That they can be spoken about in public. That they can be written down and tied to a tree, as if there is a benevolent force that cares, that will, on some other plane of existence, read your wishes. This shows a belief in kindness in the universe. It makes me uncomfortable. Must be some whispery hope hiding inside me that still longs for the tooth fairy for me to react so hostilely to anyone who dares to go around wishing. Like gamblers and lottery players, and Occupy Wall Street with their signs thinking anyone will listen and suddenly change. They enrage me. They and their hopes.

These wish trees go too far into the light!

How is it that Ono can be at once so, so dark and deep, and yet so, so bright and light and wish-y, too? Having grown up on fantasy and science fiction, I always wondered if aliens were living here right now, and we just didn't see or comprehend them because they communicated and traveled and nourished themselves on such different planes, or in such unthought-of ways, that we wouldn't be capable of seeing what was right there alongside us. I think this is how Yoko Ono is.

Cut open and covered. Personal and impersonal. Yoko's activism is not like Occupy Wall Street or gambling or the lottery. She does not invade other people's space. She invites the photographers and journalists and audience into her privacy. She tries to show that it's not actually her space or ours, because we are her. We are all gurus, and if we emanate peace, our vibrations go somewhere, have effect. People in the world who don't know they have a choice, who don't have a voice, she makes a choice herself and uses her voice herself, and somehow that could ignite something for them. It's magic, maybe. OWS is about demanding things. The lottery is about wanting things. Yoko is about showing you you already have and are everything. Her protest is not against the angry, the abusive, or the filthy rich. It's for them as much as it's for anyone. Most protest is about punishment and redistribution. Yoko doesn't even entertain those concepts.

While her art and politics appear terribly and inappropriately personal, they are in fact impersonal, in the best sense of the word. They are for the benefit of people she's never met and never will be, strangers in faraway countries, and homosexuals. Yoko has no vested interest, no profit, in the protests she launches. And they brought trouble onto her and her husband from the government and derision from the media. There was no reason for her to do it, nothing in it for her, except that she believes that it is true.

AMBASSADOR OF AUTISM

In 2010, Yoko Ono was named the first "Global Autism Ambassador."
?!
Where did that come from?
Well, autism is defined "by impairment of the ability to form normal social relationships, by impairment of the ability to communicate with others." That's pretty much Yoko Ono's career! Unwilling to be or do or say things the usual ways, she's forged her own way. I think it's society that is impaired—both in the mental health field (which is really about what forms our era's concepts of acceptable realities) and in art criticism. And in criminal prosecution and in shunning (which is really just quiet bullying), and how we deal with drug abuse, and in cold and critical parenting and the acting-out child getting the blame. Attacking the symptoms instead of the disease. I saw an old farmer get some collie dogs to do what he wanted with just the tone of his voice and the collie dogs got the sheep to do what they wanted just with their eyes. No beating, zapping, barking, nipping. Just understanding.

I think it's society that is impaired in its ability to understand certain unique relationships, and in its inability to receive strange communications. I have a son in the autism spectrum, and he just doesn't get that other people don't care about wormholes and black holes and time-space continuums because it's not real to them like it is real and present and imperative to him. He may be right and we may be all wrong. Lots of geniuses from ancient times are now guessed to have been autistic. Anyway, I see my son in Yoko's single-minded dedication to her obsessions to help other people see, and in her just not getting that other people are offended or find her methods or her interest unimportant or not real.

Many forward-thinking unusual people have been locked up, or burned, or beheaded, just for speaking up. Yoko has had her share of tribulations, too, for not fitting just right into any known categories. How she expresses is too raw; what she believes, unfinished, unknown. It's not part of the story we retell ourselves, to bring comfort, about what it means to be human. It's what we try not to know—vaginas and breasts are fine to leave out and about as art, and dictators just need love, too, and wars can be ended by lying around having beautiful thoughts.

I think I'm going to go have a beautiful thought or two now myself.

SELECTED BIBLIOGRAPHY

This list of sources is by no means a complete record of the material I consulted while writing this book. However, the works listed here served as my key references and are recommended reading for those who wish to learn more about Yoko Ono.

Clayson, Alan, with Barb Jungr and Robb Johnson. *Woman: The Incredible Life of Yoko Ono.* Surrey, UK: Chrome Dreams, 2004.

Johnstone, Nick. *Yoko Ono Talking: Yoko Ono in Her Own Words.* London: Omnibus Press, 2005.

Junod, Tom. "What I've Learned: Yoko Ono." *Esquire*, January 2011.

Ono, Yoko. *Grapefruit: A Book of Instructions and Drawings.* New York: Simon & Schuster, 2000.

Ono, Yoko. *Instruction Paintings.* Boston: Weatherhill, 1995.

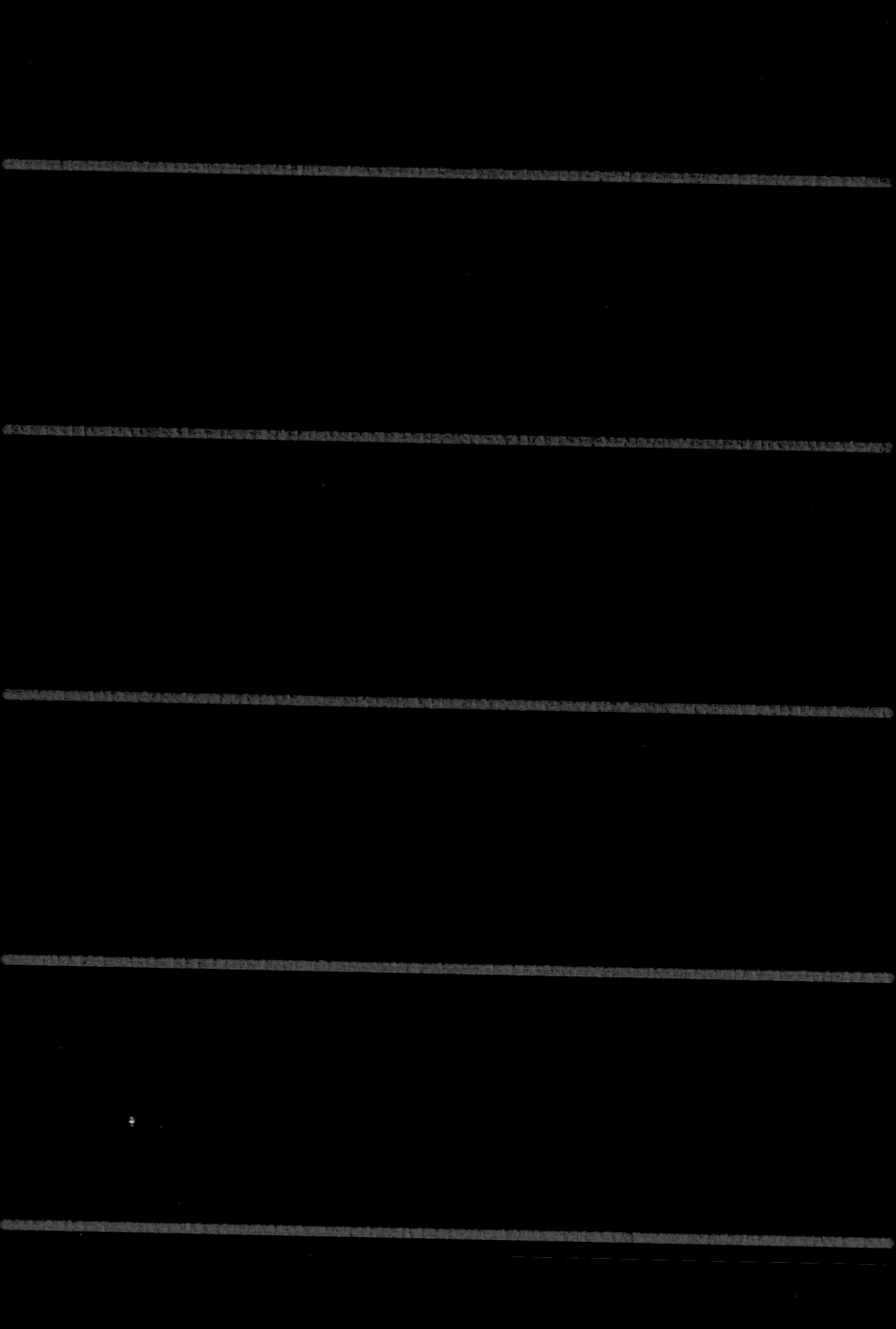